VISITING
THE NORMANDY INVASION BEACHES AND BATTLEFIELDS

BATTLEFIELDS MADE EASY

For Samantha, George and Claudia and in memory of Dad

VISITING THE NORMANDY INVASION BEACHES AND BATTLEFIELDS

BATTLEFIELDS MADE EASY

GARETH HUGHES

Pen & Sword
MILITARY

First published in Great Britain in 2019 and reprinted in 2024 by
Pen & Sword Military
an imprint of
Pen & Sword Books Ltd
47 Church Street
Barnsley
South Yorkshire
S70 2AS

Copyright © Gareth Hughes 2019, 2024

ISBN 978 1 47385 432 1

The right of Gareth Hughes to be identified as the Author of this Work has been asserted by him in accordance with the Copyright, Designs and Patents Act 1988.

A CIP catalogue record for this book is available from the British Library

All rights reserved. No part of this book may be reproduced or transmitted in any form or by any means, electronic or mechanical including photocopying, recording or by any information storage and retrieval system, without permission from the Publisher in writing.

Typeset in Ehrhardt by
Mac Style Ltd, Bridlington, East Yorkshire
Printed in the UK on paper from a sustainable source by CPI Group (UK) Ltd, Croydon, CR0 4YY

Pen & Sword Books Ltd incorporates the imprints of Pen & Sword Archaeology, Atlas, Aviation, Battleground, Discovery, Family History, History, Maritime, Military, Naval, Politics, Railways, Select, Transport, True Crime, Fiction, Frontline Books, Leo Cooper, Praetorian Press, Seaforth Publishing and Wharncliffe.

For a complete list of Pen & Sword titles please contact
PEN & SWORD BOOKS LIMITED
47 Church Street, Barnsley, South Yorkshire, S70 2AS, England
E-mail: enquiries@pen-and-sword.co.uk
Website: www.pen-and-sword.co.uk

Contents

About the Author	vi
Preface	vii
D-Day in Numbers	ix
How to use this book	x
Visiting the Normandy beaches and battlefields with a School Group	1
Army units, sizes and structure	5
The Second World War – A Timeline	7
The Second World War – A Very Brief History	13
Remembrance, Memorialisation and the Commonwealth War Graves Commission	33
D-Day: A Glossary of some Key Terms	39
Normandy and D-Day: A History	43
Tour One: Utah and Omaha	57
Tour Two: Sword, Juno and Gold	105
After D-Day	162
D-Day Museums	163
Going further, doing more	166
Further Resources and Web Links	169
Acknowledgements	171
Index	173

About the Author

Gareth Hughes is the Head of Middle School and Head of History and Politics at Pocklington School, near York. From 2011–2014 he served as Secondary Education Advisor to the British Association for American Studies. He is a sometimes public speaker, conference host and education consultant. Alongside leading school and adult groups to the battlefields, cemeteries and invasion sites of Normandy, he has led tours to multiple locations on the First World War's Western Front as well as other trips to Moscow, St Petersburg, Washington D.C., New York, Boston, Philadelphia, Alabama, Georgia, Paris, London and Munich. You might also find him, from time to time, serving up banal and trivial comments to the world on Twitter @thehistoryman.

Preface

George Henry Hughes is a name that will mean nothing to you and nor should it. He was my grandfather. In 1916 he found himself in a previously unremarkable area of northern France which I am sure will be familiar to you: the Somme. Unlike the 19,240 on the first day alone who were not so lucky, George survived the battle and the war but spent the rest of his life plagued by ill-health brought on by the wicked toll of shrapnel wounds.

My great-grandfather also served on the Western Front and in the east as part of British efforts to support the 'Whites' against the 'Reds' during the Russian Civil War. My other grandfather, stationed for a time in Iceland, hunted German submarines during the Second World War and my step-grandfather served in India during the same conflict.

In 1995 I first visited the battlefields of the Great War as a fourteen-year-old student. The experience was humbling, emotional and ultimately life-changing. Two years later I first visited the Normandy coastline and, once again, was stunned by the deeds of men who traversed that ground years before.

Whether it be to First or Second World War sites, these are pilgrimages that I have subsequently taken every year since becoming a teacher, taking hundreds of students around France and Belgium, both as an accompaniment to their history studies and, more importantly, as a wider aid to their human understanding.

This book is the distillation of some of that experience. It is not meant to be exhaustive, nor even a full tour guide. There are many great sites and memorials that do not make it into these pages. What it is, however, is the highlight reel.

This book is primarily written for secondary school history departments who wish to undertake a one to four-day tour of some of the iconic sites of the Normandy D-Day invasion area. However, it will also be of interest and use to the inexperienced and perhaps first time general visitor. The major focus is on the five landing beaches, with a few suggestions for those looking to go a little further afield and wishing to take in more museums as well. The book is aimed largely at the non-expert departments (i.e. History Departments that do not specialize in this area, have not taken these trips before or who have previously relied upon tour guides whilst abroad); but it will also be useful to those departments that are more confident and experienced as a single volume 'pick-up-and-deliver' resource.

Many colleagues I know have felt incredibly daunted when trying to devise their own itinerary and tour due to the array of sites and guide books/histories on the market. As the number of books on the D-Day landings has proliferated, so has the concentrated focus on niche areas. This book is an attempt to strip away some of that level of detail, all quite brilliant for the battlefield expert but too much for the teacher tour leader, and package a tour that teachers can deliver and students will enjoy.

When visiting Normandy, students can struggle to differentiate between or lose track of the different beaches and sectors, especially when you make multiple stops. In this book I have tried to build visits around individual stories just as much as the sites themselves, so that even if the details are forgotten, the memorable narratives should remain.

Therefore, I make no apologies for leaving out some details that an expert would deem vital, such as the movements of regiments or battalions, unless I felt them essential in enhancing the understanding of a particular visit for the expected type of audience. This is not meant to be a definitive military history; the main aim is to provide context, narrative and a gripping experience, which will hopefully then inspire the individual to carry out reading and research of their own and spark an interest for life.

Quite simply, my hope is that this book gives you all you need to deliver and experience a moving, entertaining and memorable trip.

For the individual visitor this book will enable you to get a good grasp of the key areas and history through a few accessible itineraries for self-touring.

Finally, I must pay my debt to the masters of the battlefield touring genre. If it were not for the outstanding and numerous publications by Major and Mrs Holt, the Battleground Europe series and the magnificent *Before Endeavours Fade* by Rose Coombs, then my own ventures across both the Western Front and Normandy would simply not have happened. This book is where you start your journey – their books are where you master it.

Gareth Hughes, Pocklington, February 2019.

D-Day in Numbers

156,115	–	number of Allied troops landed in Normandy
10,250	–	Allied casualties
4,000–9,000	–	estimated number of German casualties
11,590	–	aircraft used by the Allies to support the landing
127	–	aircraft lost by the Allies
6,939	–	naval vessels used in Operation Neptune
104,428	–	tons of supplies landed by D+5
50	–	Field Marshal Rommel, the man tasked with defending Northern France, was in Germany on 6 June, celebrating his wife's milestone birthday
7 million	–	the cost (£) of filming the Omaha Beach scene in Saving Private Ryan
4.5	–	width in miles of Omaha Beach
45	–	Allied casualties per machine gun on Sword Beach
12	–	Allied casualties per machine gun on Utah Beach
15	–	percentage of paratroopers that landed in their planned drop zone
1,500	–	trains destroyed by the French Resistance and Allied bombing prior to D-Day
2,500,000	–	the number of troops that would pass through the Mulberry Harbour in the ten months following D-Day

How to use this book

In this guide there are two main itineraries: Tour One largely focuses on American operations whilst Tour Two follows the British and Canadian story. They are designed to cover one full day each but contain optional extra stops and suggestions that enable you to extend them over another day or two. Because there are so many excellent museums in the area, it is possible to spend many more days visiting these; I have suggested a few in the main itinerary but have also included a more comprehensive list so that you are able to pick and choose depending on the time available, their location and your particular interest.

The itineraries give you a realistic number of visits for a day with a group. If you are using this book as an individual or small group then you might find that you spend longer at each site as you are not having to 'stage-manage' the visits in any way. The most common mistake for schools and general visitors trying to do their own trip without a tour guide is to cram too much in – it is also the same mistake that enthusiastic and knowledgeable tourists make too. I have certainly had to learn to limit my own itineraries. I have also endeavoured to avoid 'cemetery fatigue', which is a particular threat to student groups.

At each site there is information which relates to:

- Context of the location
- Your orientation (where relevant)
- Narrative – the most crucial part! Essentially, the history and stories to engage and entertain your charges with. Or, for the individual using this guide, the information to help you to understand each visit.
- Activity (where relevant).
- Any relevant photographs and maps. However, I would also recommend purchasing Major and Mrs Holt's Battle Maps of the Normandy D-Day landing beaches alongside a good road map.

Along the way there will be tips for lunch breaks, free time possibilities for students and other helpful pointers.

Sentences written in *italics* are directions or instructions to you.

Visiting the Normandy beaches and battlefields with a School Group

Although this book can be used by the individual traveller, be this their first time in Normandy or a veteran of such ventures, when I originally conceived the idea for this book it was with large groups or school tours in mind. Therefore, these next few short paragraphs are intended for anyone leading a group. If you have the good fortune to be neither a teacher nor leading a group around the sites, then please do skip this section.

* * *

Why do it?

Well, this question is probably redundant if you have gone to the trouble of buying this book. For value for money, curriculum content, enjoyment and overall impact on the students, you will have trouble finding a better trip.

Which age groups should I take?

The simple answer is any, although I would recommend not younger that Year 9. I have taken mixed groups ranging from 13–18 and GCSE only. I have taken trips which are solely pitched as an 'interest' trip and those which are linked to specific curriculum study. Personally, the freedom of the 'interest' trips, where those students on the trip are there because they already have an interest in the war, makes the venture usually more enjoyable.

How do I go about booking it?

It is a simple conundrum: to tour company or to not tour company? Based in the north of England, I favour using a tour company, simply because they have the ability to get better deals on the ferry crossing than I can usually do and this outweighs the (relatively small) additional costs which they charge in order to make some profit. My trips tend to be relatively long compared to many; five or six days is the norm, sometimes mixed between various locations i.e. Normandy and Ypres (to study the Great War). However, if I were based in the south, and taking a one or two day trip, then it is relatively straightforward to book without a tour company and still obtain good prices on whichever crossing route you favour. Do note, however, that many schools require you to use a tour company

in order to ensure that the trip is ABTA, ABTOT and/or ATOL protected. Check your school's policies to be safe.

A note on ferry crossings; I know many teachers who fear the overnight crossings. I have done both the short crossing and the overnight ones and by a large margin I prefer the overnight crossing. The students love them and it adds an extra something to the trip as a whole. You just have to be tight on where students are allowed to go (e.g. not outside on deck without a teacher) and on regular meeting-up times. However, most school groups heading to Normandy will probably take the short Dover-Calais route via coach and drive down to the area from there. If you can get a reasonable price, the Portsmouth-Caen route is excellent: it enables you to visit the superb D-Day museum in Portsmouth, in order to set the context of the trip; when you arrive in France you are in the Sword Beach sector and just minutes from Pegasus Bridge.

The main considerations to make are: how much of the booking process do you feel comfortable handling; and how much of the trip will you lead yourself? If you decide not to use a tour company, then you must also check with your insurance that the cover will support your actions as a tour operator.

I have never been before – do I need a guide?

You have this book! However, if you cannot get out to France for a pre-trip recce so that you can visit the places and get a feel for how to deliver the tour, perhaps you should use a tour guide on your first trip whilst reading this book along the way. In future years you will be able to take the trip yourself and save on the added cost of hiring guides.

What processes, risk assessments, pre-trip planning requires carrying out?

This will very much depend on your school policies. In general, you will have to seek permission to run the trip, put out letters of interest to the students, reserve your accommodation and travel whilst collecting deposits, fill out risk assessments, collect all monies and host an information evening for parents. However, the first port of call is

your Director of Activities/Co-Curriculum/Educational Visits and your school policies. Do not let the paper work put you off; the trip is more than worth it!

Where should I stay with the group?

Now this is another conundrum. In my previous book on the Somme and Ypres I was able to recommend, with confidence, a number of places. However, I will be honest and admit that I have not found the standard of service to be up to the same mark in the Normandy region for school groups. I have wondered why some of these places allow school groups to stay, given their obvious disdain for children! I have also found it to be the case, unfortunately, that food provision can leave something to be desired. So, in a nutshell, I hope you find outstanding accommodation that works well for your group – if you do, please can you let me know?

Coach Travel

This can make your life easy… or absolute hell. Please, whatever else you do, ask for a driver who knows the area! It is relatively straightforward to traverse the various locations in comparison to many First World War sites; but you do have numerous other things to worry about whilst abroad – the last thing you need is to be map reading for someone who has never left the UK before (which has happened to me). Although now fairly common, I would urge you to pay the extra (relatively minor) cost to get a luxury coach (leg room and a toilet).

What should I take with me?

Although I would like to think that this book will suffice for leading a tour, your interest is likely to grow over the years and you will want to develop your own unique tour, bringing in new stops along the way. You will probably wish to take a selection of good books with you to help. See the further resources section of this book to get you started.

It is a good idea to take a healthy supply of remembrance crosses with you so that students can leave them at headstones/sites as they wish. You may also wish to lay a wreath too. Visit http://www.britishlegion.org.uk/ to order crosses/wreaths.

In the last few years I have found the addition of a tablet device extremely useful. On this you can store relevant images of individuals, maps, battle photographs, audio and visual content.

DVDs for the coach are obviously a good idea too.

Any tips?

Start your days early, build in toilet stops and some free time and end at a reasonable time so that the students can relax a little too. If you stay in a hotel near to the beaches themselves then your evening activities will often be hours of beach cricket/rugby/football.

If the weather is wet – and it can be even in summer – make sure students have brought waterproofs with them and a change of footwear so that muddy boots can be left in the coach luggage compartment.

The main point is to be flexible. Too many tour leaders try to stick to their itinerary throughout and ignore the obvious signs when a group starts to flag. Have a few contingency visits up your sleeve and try to build in an overarching theme to each day so that the students have something to grasp on to throughout. It is a good idea for them to have a guide to the trip too, something that they can read on the coach.

I do not tend to go for the worksheet route when visiting sites. This is simply personal preference; I have, however, witnessed several brilliant uses of such material. Ideas for these could be to collate designs of cap badges, follow particular regiments or old boys of the school, mapping battlefield sites or for considering unique aspects of the burials in a particular cemetery. You can, of course, make them to fit whatever task you need.

When planning, do factor in a little extra cash for emergencies and/or treats – it is amazing what the offer of an ice-cream can do for a weary group of teenagers.

Finally, make sure you build in time for a drink of an evening; you will deserve it! Enjoy.

* * *

Army units, sizes and structure

One of the most confusing aspects of warfare, for those of us relatively unfamiliar with the terminology and military organisations, can be that of specific formation or unit sizes. Below is a simplified look at the composition of the British, American and German infantry units during the Second World War.[1]

Formation/Unit	Consisting of	Number of men	Commanded by
Section	–	c. 5–12	Sergeant/Corporal
Squad	2+ Sections	c. 10–25	Sergeant
Platoon/Troop	2+ Squads	c. 20–50	1st Lieutenant
Company	2+ Platoons/Troops	c. 100–250	Captain/Major
Battalion	3+ Companies	c. 400–1,100	Lieutenant Colonel
Regiment	2+ Battalions	c. 1,000–2,000	Colonel/Brigadier
Brigade	3+ Battalions	c. 1,500–3,500	Major General/Brigadier/Colonel
Division	3+ Brigades/Regiments	c. 10,000–15,000	Lieutenant General/Major General
Corps	2+ Divisions	c. 25,000–50,000	General/Lieutenant General
Army	2+ Corps	c. 100,000–150,000	Field Marshal/General

The discrepancy in numbers, particularly in the largest formations, is due to how large the support and other fighting arms were, e.g. artillery, engineers, medical, admin, signals, headquarters, etc. The basic reason for breaking armies down into units is to streamline command and control.

A regiment in the British army, in particular the infantry, is not usually a single unit or battalion. It is a historic designation, such as the Black Watch or the Green Howards. With multiple battalions, in a particular regiment, men could be serving in theatres all over the world simultaneously.

When units went into battle, they were rarely at full strength. Either due to illness, injury, leave or death, numbers would be depleted. Also, the major combatant nations had several 'armies' within their overall military structure. Sometimes armies would be combined into Army Groups to create large forces for major operations. For example, the

6 *Visiting the Normandy Invasion Beaches and Battlefields*

21st Army Group, headed by General (later Field Marshal) Bernard 'Monty' Montgomery, controlled all ground forces in the initial stages of Operation Overlord, thus commanding British, Canadian, Polish and American[2] troops during the landing.

U.S., British and Canadian infantry divisions ranged in size from 15,000–20,000 troops on D-Day. Allied airborne divisions were roughly half that size, whilst German divisions typically contained fewer than 10,000 men.

Footnotes:

1. These three combatant nations were organised along roughly similar lines. However, this is a simplified table and not all would use the same designation/nomenclature.
2. Once enough U.S. forces had landed, the Americans then formed their own Army Group, consisting of four field armies.

The Second World War – A Timeline

1939	
1 September	Germany invades Poland
3 September	Britain, France, Australia and New Zealand declare war on Germany
5 September	USA declares neutrality
10 September	Canada declares war on Germany; the Battle of the Atlantic begins
17 September	Soviet Union invades Poland
27 September	Poland surrenders to Germany
29 September	Germany and the Soviet Union divide up Poland
30 November	Soviet Union invades Finland

1940	
8 January	Beginning of rationing in Britain
16 March	Scapa Flow naval base bombed
9 April	Germany invades Denmark and Norway
10 May	German invasions of France, Belgium, Luxembourg and the Netherlands. On the same day, Winston Churchill becomes Prime Minister
26 May–3 June	Evacuation from Dunkirk of Allied forces
10 June	Italy declares war on Britain and France
14 June	Germany takes control of Paris
22 June	France signs an armistice with Germany
10 July	The Battle of Britain begins
13 August	Luftwaffe bombing of airfields and factories in England commences
23/24 August	First German air raids on London
25/26 August	First British air raids on Berlin

7 September	The Blitz – mainly on London – begins
13 September	Italy invades Egypt
27 September	The Axis Pact signed by Germany, Italy and Japan
7 October	German forces enter Romania
12 October	Germany postpones Operation Sea Lion (planned invasion of Britain)
28 October	Italy invades Greece
20 November	Hungary joins the Axis
23 November	Romania joins the Axis
9 December	British offensive in North Africa against Italy begins
1941	
22 January	British and Australian forces victorious in Tobruk, North Africa
11 February	British advances in Italian Somaliland, East Africa
12 February	General Erwin Rommel arrives in North Africa
14 February	German Afrika Korps begins to arrive in North Africa
7 March	British forces arrive in Greece
11 March	The Lend-Lease Act is signed between the USA and Britain
6 April	German invasions of Greece and Yugoslavia
14 April	German attacks on Tobruk
17 April	Yugoslavia surrenders to Germany
27 April	Greece surrenders to Germany
1 May	German attack on Tobruk resisted
22 June	German invasion of the Soviet Union begins – Operation Barbarossa
12 July	Britain and Soviet Union agree Mutual Assistance
14 August	Roosevelt and Churchill agree the Atlantic Charter
20 August	German assault on Leningrad begins
3 September	First use of gas chamber in Auschwitz concentration camp
September-November	Major German advances in the Soviet Union: Odessa, Kharkov, Sevastopol, Rostov
2 October	German advance on Moscow underway
27 November	Soviet troops drive German forces from Rostov
5 December	German forces abandon Moscow advance

6 December	Soviet counter-offensive launched from Moscow
7 December	Japan attack US Naval base at Pearl Harbor
8 December	The USA and Britain declare war on Japan
11 December	Germany declares war on the USA
19 December	Adolf Hitler consolidates German Army so as to be fully under his control

1942	
1 January	United Nations Declaration signed by Allied Nations
13 January	German U-boat attacks begin along the east coast of the USA
20 January	Wannsee Conference – leading Nazis meet to decide the 'Final Solution' to the Jewish question
26 January	American troops begin to arrive in Britain
May	Large German offensive undertaken in the Crimea
July	First Battle of El Alamein
9 July	German advance towards Stalingrad underway
22 July	Deportations from the Warsaw Ghetto begin
2 September	Rommel's forces driven back in North Africa by Montgomery's Eighth Army
13 September	Battle of Stalingrad begins
1 November	Axis lines broken at El Alamein
8 November	Operation Torch begins – US invasion of North Africa
11 November	German and Italian occupation of Vichy France
19 November	Soviet counter-offensives at Stalingrad begin
16 December	Soviet forces defeat Italian troops on the River Don, USSR

1943	
2 January	Beginning of German withdrawal from the Caucasus
10 January	Major Soviet assault against German forces in Stalingrad
14–24 January	Casablanca Conference – Allied strategy committed to ending the war through absolute and unconditional surrender of Germany, Japan and Italy
23 January	Montgomery's Eighth Army captures Tripoli
2 February	German troops surrender at Stalingrad

8 February	Soviet forces take Kursk
2 March	German forces begin to withdraw from Tunisia
19 April	Beginning of the Warsaw Ghetto uprising
7 May	Allies take Tunisia
13 May	German and Italian forces surrender in North Africa
16 May	End of Jewish resistance in the Warsaw Ghetto
22 May	German U-boat operations suspended in the Atlantic
11 June	Liquidation of all Jewish ghettos in Poland instigated
10 July	Allied landings in Sicily
19 July	Rome bombed by Allies
22 July	US forces capture Palermo, Sicily
25 July	Mussolini removed from power and arrested; Fascist government collapses
28 July	Massive Allied bombing creates fire-storm in Hamburg
12–17 August	German forces evacuate from Sicily
8 September	Italian surrender announced
9 September	Allied landings: Salerno and Taranto
11 September	German forces occupy Rome
12 September	German rescue of Mussolini
23 September	Mussolini re-establishes control; Fascist government restored
1 October	Allies enter Naples
13 October	Italy, under General Badoglio's anti-fascist government, declares war on Germany
6 November	Soviet recapture of Kiev
28 November	Roosevelt, Churchill and Stalin meet at the Tehran Conference to discuss the opening of a second front against Germany
24–26 December	Major Soviet offensives on the Ukrainian Front

1944

6 January	Soviets advance into Poland
17 January	First Allied attack at Monte Cassino
22 January	Allied landings at Anzio, Italy
27 January	Leningrad siege ends

15–18 February	Allied bombing of Monte Cassino monastery
16 February	German counter-attack at Anzio
15 March	Second Allied attack at Monte Cassino
9 May	Soviet forces recapture Sevastopol, Crimea
12 May	German surrender in the Crimea
15 May	German withdrawal to the Adolf Hitler Line, central Italy
25 May	German retreat from Anzio
5 June	Allies enter Rome
6 June	D-Day landings at Normandy, France
13 June	First German V-1 rockets launched against Britain
9 July	British and Canadian troops capture Caen
18 July	American troops enter St. Lô
20 July	Failed Wolf's Lair assassination attempt on Adolf Hitler by German Army officers – the Stauffenberg Plot
28 July	Soviet forces capture Brest-Litovsk. US troops take Coutances, France
1 August	Polish Home Army uprising against German Army in Warsaw; US troops reach Avranches, France
7 August	German counter-offensive at Avranches
15 August	Operation Dragoon launched (Allied landings in Southern France)
19 August	French Resistance uprising in Paris; Soviet assault in the Balkans begins
20 August	Allied forces encircle Germans in the Falaise Pocket, France
25 August	Liberation of Paris
4 September	Finland and USSR agree a ceasefire
13 September	US forces reach the Siegfried Line in Western Germany
17 September	Operation Market Garden – Allied airborne attack on Holland – begins
26 September	Soviet forces occupy Estonia
2 October	Polish Home Army surrenders to German troops
2–21 October	Battle of Aachen; the first city on German soil to be captured by Allied forces. Over 5,000 German soldiers taken prisoner by US troops
14 October	Allies liberate Athens, Greece; General Erwin Rommel forced suicide
30 October	Final use of the gas chambers in Auschwitz
20 November	French forces reach the Rhine
16–27 December	Battle of the Bulge, a major German surprise counter-offensive in the Ardennes region

1945	
1–17 January	German withdrawal from the Ardennes
17 January	Soviet forces capture Warsaw
26 January	Soviet troops liberate Auschwitz
4–11 February	Roosevelt, Churchill and Stalin meet at the Yalta Conference to discuss post-war Europe
13–14 February	Allied bombing destruction of Dresden
7 March	Allies capture Cologne
30 March	Soviet forces capture Danzig
1 April	US troops encircle German forces in the Ruhr
12 April	President Roosevelt dies; Harry Truman is the new President
16 April	Soviet's undertake final assault on Berlin
18 April	German forces surrender in the Ruhr
21 April	Soviets enter Berlin
28 April	Mussolini captured and hanged by Italian partisans
30 April	Adolf Hitler commits suicide
2 May	German troops in Italy surrender
7 May	Unconditional German surrender to Allies
8 May	Victory in Europe Day
5 June	Allies take control over German government
26 June	United Nations Charter signed in San Francisco
1 July	British, American and French troops join Soviet forces in occupying Berlin
16 July	Potsdam Conference – Truman, British PM Clement Attlee and Stalin meet to discuss the conclusion of the war with Japan and post-war Europe
6 August	Atomic bomb dropped on Hiroshima, Japan
8 August	USSR declares war on Japan, invades Manchuria
9 August	Atomic bomb dropped on Nagasaki, Japan
15 August	Unconditional surrender of Japan
2 September	Japanese sign surrender; Victory over Japan Day
24 October	The United Nations comes into existence
20 November	Leading Nazis put on trial at Nuremberg

The Second World War – A Very Brief History

Causes

In the West, in the decades following the end of the Second World War, the conventional explanation for the outbreak of the conflict has largely settled upon that of an evil Nazi regime, led by a deranged racist bile-spewing lunatic, exploiting the weak Allied policy of appeasement in order to unleash a global conflict that: a) would overturn the terms of the harsh Treaty of Versailles and b) expand and entrench an ethnically pure Third Reich[1] across Europe.

Although it is far beyond the remit of this book to critically examine this, it is important that we consider a little more perspective and context so that we may better understand the complex set of events and ideas that led to this war. To place the full explanation on the motives of the Third Reich runs the risk of viewing history through the lens of what we now know rather than the reality of the situation as it actually unfolded. The causes of this war were many and complex. They were deeply rooted yet simultaneously reactionary and involved numerous competing world views and the power of the forces of history.

The First World War

Before considering the epoch-shattering 1914–1918 cataclysm it is worth going back to the formation of Germany itself and the defining 1870–1871 Franco-Prussian War. Following the defeat of France, the new German state, finally proclaimed on 18 January 1871, could define itself as a nation forged out of conflict and subsequent victory, walking with the strutting confidence of the Prussian military class, who dominated the political make-up of the new nation.

The Balance of Power in Europe was a concept crucial for nineteenth century statesmen; simply, no one power should be allowed to dominate the continent and keeping a relative peace was built upon this crucial doctrine. In truth, following the defeat of Napoleon, it was the British who had a vested interest in maintaining this – the emergence of a newly powerful, growing rival was not good news for London.

Otto von Bismarck, the great German statesman, dominated German foreign policy from 1862 until his removal from office in March 1890 by the young Emperor Wilhelm II. Bismarck had managed to feed the development of German industrial power and might whilst reassuring the rest of Europe, through cautious diplomacy and *Realpolitik*, that there was nothing to fear from this new Great Power. It was the man who removed him from office who bears a great burden of responsibility for what would follow.

Ever since 1888, Germany had been ruled by the unstable, jealous and distinctly odd Kaiser Wilhelm II. He believed, as did many of his people, that the acquisition of colonies would be the symbol of achieving real world power. *Weltpolitik* was the new language and, in reality, it meant a world mission for Germany; a mission to achieve the status that her industrial, technological, military and cultural achievements merited. Many of these same beliefs would be at the core of Adolf Hitler's political thinking too.

Alliances were the diplomatic trend in the late nineteenth and early twentieth centuries; designed to ensure parity and a balance of power on the continent; they would, in fact, deliver nothing of the sort. These alliances shifted and fluctuated over time, but by 1914 the delineation was clear. On one side, Germany and Austria-Hungary, to be joined by the Ottomans and other opportunistic nations along the way. France and Russia allied themselves in a defensive partnership. Belgium remained neutral, with a guarantee of its position by the Treaty of London of 1839, signed by all the Great Powers, including Great Britain. Finally, in one of the most remarkable realignments in modern history, France and Great Britain agreed an *Entente Cordiale* in 1904.

Archduke Franz Ferdinand, heir to the throne of Austria–Hungary, had married the Czech Countess, Sophie Chotek, in 1900. In 1914, on their wedding anniversary, they travelled to a fractious part of the Austro-Hungarian Empire, Bosnia, to inspect the army in Sarajevo.

Nationalism was rife in the Balkans and was a continuing source of political strife and occasional war. The people of Bosnia-Herzegovina were a mix of Bosnians, Slavs and Croats. A Serbian minority itched to break away and join their homeland.

On 28 June, after already surviving one assassination attempt that day from the Serbian nationalist 'Black Hand' secret society, the Archduke's car took a wrong turning. A young student and member of the 'Black Hand', Gavrilo Princip, took advantage of his opportunity, raised his pistol and shot dead Franz Ferdinand and Sophie, with her unborn child, as they sat beside each other in the rear of the car.

Diplomatic dominoes tumbled, alliances were invoked and the Great War was underway.

Throughout the Great War, Germany was successful at the type of warfare that she had not planned on waging – that of a defensive strategy, once the war of movement had coughed and spluttered to a muddy halt. The much heralded German Schlieffen Plan had turned out to be one of the greatest failures in military history, ensuring a long, drawn-out war of attrition rather than the short and sharp victory envisaged in the plan. A mixture of years of meddling (and weakening) the plan, unexpectedly resilient Belgian resistance, the decision of Britain to observe the Treaty of London in defence of Belgium and the swift Russian mobilisation in the East which led to the splitting of German forces, France's Plan XVII invasion into Germany and, eventually, the cold winter of 1914 brought about its failure and meant that a very different type of war would uncoil in all its grim and bloody incarnations. This was a war that used modern industrial and chemical weaponry on a scale never seen before. It was also a war of brutal savagery.

Germany did enjoy a successful 1915 but only came anything like close to winning the war with the massive Kaiser's Offensives of 1918 – but this was such a last-ditch and risky gamble that it ultimately hastened her defeat.

The Peace

It is difficult to overstate the impact of the Great War, whether it be from the millions killed and mutilated to the redrawing of the map of Europe, the collapse of former great Empires to the birth of a major Communist nation, the social and economic impact to the destabilising ending of the balance of power – this war was like no other. What can be stated, however, is that the peace settlement failed in numerous respects, perhaps above all as regards Germany.

When the Treaty of Versailles was signed on 28 June 1919, officially ending the war and placing onerous terms upon Germany, a great many of the seeds of the Second World War were sown.

Key articles from the treaty:

- 1–26: Germany was forbidden from joining the new League of Nations
- 42: The Rhineland was demilitarised
- 45: The Saar, an area full of lucrative coalfields, was transferred into French possession for 15 years
- 51: The disputed region of Alsace-Lorraine was returned to France
- 80: Anschluss (German unification with Austria) forbidden
- 87: Territory in eastern Germany given to Poland
- 119: German colonies given to France and Britain under the mandate system
- 160: The German army restricted to 100,000 men
- 181: The German navy restricted to six battleships and no submarines
- 198: The German air force disbanded and forbidden
- 231: Germany was declared responsible for the loss, damage and destruction caused by the war
- 232: Germany would pay reparations for the damage caused by the war.

Although the Social Democrat government, bundled into power on 9 November 1918 due to the collapse of the German military and the abdication of the Kaiser, had expected (and were accepting of the fact) that Germany would have to pay reparations, the final sum of 132 billion Marks ($31.4 billion or £6.6 billion)[2] came as a blow. However, it was article 231, the 'war guilt' clause, that was received with most opprobrium by German politicians and people alike. In order to justify the reparations, the Allies instructed Germany to accept full responsibility for the war. This suggested a moral blame for the war for which the victorious nations now shared no responsibility. Given also that German representatives were not allowed to attend negotiations but only to respond in writing, it is no wonder that, very soon after the ink was dry, in Germany the treaty became known as the 'Diktat'. The German Republic was born – but in truth it was a sickly child with poor life prospects.

In that political masterpiece, *The Prince*, Niccolo Machiavelli advised that a defeated foe 'must be either pampered or crushed'. The crucial problem with the Treaty of Versailles was that it achieved neither; it managed to humiliate Germany but not annihilate her.

Germany did lose just short of 14 per cent of her territory, most of this to Poland and France. Due to this and the loss of seven million people who went with the land, German economic productivity fell by 13.5 per cent. Alongside the reparations, neutered military might and the infamous war guilt clause, this does seem, at first glance, quite harsh treatment. However, if you were to look at the terms that Germany placed upon Russia in 1918 or, in fact, the total capitulation, occupation and re-imagining of Germany that the Allies placed upon her in 1945 then, one can conclude, that Versailles was not that punitive after all.

To analyse what went wrong with the peace, it is essential to note that the German army was permitted to march home, carrying its weaponry and cheered on by fellow country folk from German town to German town – flowers and kisses reigning down upon these brothers, sons and husbands. This did not look like a defeated army. It is important to remember that the German people had been indoctrinated for years with the news that they were just one push away from all-out victory. So what conspiracy was this? This army looked far from done. Who was responsible for this humiliation?

Many in Germany had also assumed (hoped?) that the peace would be drawn up using American President Woodrow Wilson's liberal-internationalist Fourteen Points as a guiding principle. But where was this sentiment in the final document? Well, for one thing, the Fourteen Points was very much *Wilson's* agenda, not Britain's and France's. For Germany to claim foul on this point was self-delusion. Those who claimed that they had accepted the Armistice based upon the understanding of the Fourteen Points conveniently forgot that they had clearly lost the war and were in little position to fight on. Indeed, it was the American General, John J. 'Black Jack' Pershing, who was the leading voice calling for the Allies to fight on in November 1918 in order to smash the German army back across its borders and into oblivion.

This bastardised peace settlement was the inevitable outcome of a situation where the victors themselves have a competing set of guiding principles and wishes. French Prime Minister Georges 'The Tiger' Clemenceau, carried by his vengeful electors, wanted the most severe of punishments. Wilson was – as he could be, given the lack of domestic impact of the war in the USA – more eager to take an enlightened post-war view, keen to allow Germany a route back to stability and acceptance. British PM Lloyd George felt the pressure of an angry nation, keen for Germany to suffer, and had to walk a tightrope between the need to please his voters whilst also following his instinct not to annihilate Germany completely. Although highly unlikely at the time, a treaty that limited German military power but enabled economic recovery would have been the ideal outcome – given that, as we shall see, many of the more punitive aspects of the treaty were redrawn, tinkered with or ignored in the 1920s; clearly the initial treaty was far from perfect. European liberal-élite guilt, plus the immense impact of John Maynard Keynes's book, *The Economic Consequences of the Peace,* shaped the general perception throughout the decade following the war that Germany had somehow been mistreated or, at least, mishandled.

Apart from the west bank of the Rhine – where American, British and French troops occupied German territory – the vast majority of Germans never had to look into the cold, harsh face of defeat. If an occupation of Germany, even limited in scale and scope, had taken place then perhaps this genuine annihilation may have been felt more thoroughly than it was. In any case, history did not go that way and early ideas that Germany had been 'stabbed in the back' by a conspiracy (the Socialist government? The Jews?) flourished. A few years later, Adolf Hitler would tap back into this sentiment, one which he hammered relentlessly in his rise to power.

'Pamper or crush'. If only someone had passed a copy of *The Prince* around the delegates at Versailles.

Crisis years to Golden Years

By the end of 1919 the new German Republic had not only agreed to the terms of the Treaty of Versailles, but had come through several periods of immense political instability during which rival groups on the left competed for pre-eminence. There was a genuine fear that Germany could follow the direction of Bolshevik Russia and undergo a Communist uprising. This fear was shown to be well founded when the Communist 'Spartacist' group attempted a *coup* in Berlin in January 1919. However, Chancellor Friedrich Ebert had previously made a controversial deal with the army commander, General Groener, to put down any *coup*. A newly formed volunteer paramilitary organisation, the *Freikorps*, largely made up of Great War veterans, carried out a bloody suppression both of this and a further left wing revolt in Munich in April, when a 'Soviet' briefly held power in Bavaria. Thus, although the Republic survived, it had done so through an ominous deal with military forces whose loyalty could not be relied upon.

In August 1919 a new constitution was adopted. At its heart was a considerable development in democratic constitutional government for Germany. The Reichstag (the national legislature), elected by proportional representation by all men and women over the age of 21, was given the authority of the state. The head of state was the President but he was subordinate to the Reichstag unless, crucially, in a national emergency, when special powers could be temporarily used by invoking Article 48 of the constitution: *'In the event that the public order and security are seriously disturbed or endangered, the Reich President may take the measures necessary for their restoration.'* This provision would be used so frequently that the Germans became accustomed to authoritarian use of centralised power; this is a critical point when considering why the actions of Adolf Hitler were not viewed as being so abnormal in a country that was, at least on paper, a constitutional democracy. Finally, the Chancellor was the head of the government, supported by a majority in the Reichstag and appointed directly by the President.

By the end of 1919, the Republic had seen off extremist threats and had developed a constitutional framework. Given the tumultuous conditions that gave birth to it, the big question was whether this new Germany could survive in the long term. Over the following fourteen years there would be crisis, recovery and then, finally and fatally, catastrophe.

The devaluation of the German currency, the *Reichsmark*, began during the Great War. The currency's situation worsened following the end of the conflict due to the demobilisation of the returning armed forces and the vast sums of money that were needed to be paid under the terms of the Treaty of Versailles. Long before the modern term of 'quantitative easing' was adopted to mask the reality of the process, the Republic turned to mass printing of new paper money in an attempt to ease the financial woes of the nation. Furthermore, as a consequence of a German default on timber deliveries in December 1922, French and Belgian forces occupied the coal, iron and steel producing Ruhr valley. Although carried out ostensibly because of the default, the Franco-Belgian authorities knew that German currency was becoming increasingly worthless and extracting reparations in resources would be more beneficial.

To add to the already inflation-ridden German economy, more paper money was printed in order to pay striking German workers in the Ruhr, who were carrying out acts of passive resistance against the occupation forces. The German economy went into free-fall and hyper-inflation followed. In November 1923 a solitary British pound was worth 16,000 million German marks. People's savings were wiped out and medieval barter temporarily returned. The German (Weimar) Republic was on the verge of collapse.[3] Political problems surfaced, with a far right *coup* in Berlin that failed in 1920 (the Kapp Putsch) and, in 1923, a doomed putsch was attempted in Munich... led by the relatively unknown Adolf Hitler.

However, a return to recovery was swift.

1923–29 was a period of revival, international rehabilitation and much needed political stability for Germany. Much praise for this situation is due to Gustav Stresemann, Chancellor in 1923 and then Foreign Minister until 1929. Under his leadership the German currency crisis was fixed by replacing the *Reichsmark* with the *Rentenmark* and negotiating an important agreement on reparations payment, known as the Dawes Plan. Following this, huge investment from the USA poured into Germany, helping to fuel an industrial revival. By 1927 overall production levels were once again at pre-Great War levels. On the international front, Germany signed a collective defence pact at Locarno in 1925 and then entered the League of Nations in 1926. *Erfüllungspolitik,* or fulfilment, was the guiding principle of Gustav Streseman. Fulfilment meant the implementation of the post-war terms in order to, eventually, return to national sovereignty and autonomy. Although deeply resented by many German people, this policy was clearly working by the end of the 1920s: in 1929 the Young Plan further reduced the amount of reparations payments required; in January 1926 the British carried out the first major reduction of occupying forces as troops left Cologne; the Inter-Allied Control Commission (a post-war watchdog) left in 1927; French troops withdrew in 1929. Germany was almost ready to function free from the shackles of military defeat and its crippling consequences.

And then came the crash...

> 'Germany is dancing on a volcano. If the short-term credits are called in a large section of our economy would collapse.'
>
> Gustav Stresemann, 1928.

Not only was Stresemann correct in his warnings but when the economic fire-storm erupted, he – arguably the most talented politician of his time – would not be around to help his country. He died on 3 October 1929 at the young age of fifty-one. On 24 October, the Wall Street stock market crash triggered off a global financial meltdown.

Loans were called in, American capital investment into Europe collapsed and nations began to protect their economies. The optimism and feeling of European co-operation and unity quickly vanished, giving rise instead to the growth of extremism and fear. Germany, despite her international rebirth, had always struggled with unemployment post-war; but now the issue snowballed. From having one and a half million unemployed in 1926, six million would be jobless by 1932. The political impact of this was widespread, deep and ultimately tragic.

Nazi Party comes to power

The German Workers' Party was formed by Anton Drexler in Munich in 1919. In September of that year, a young Austrian, bitter at the outcome of the war and brimming with anger, joined it. Adolf Hitler became leader of the now National Socialist German Workers' Party (NSDAP), or Nazis, in July 1921. The party centralised its organisation in Munich and used violent tactics, deploying a horde of rough bully-boy paramilitaries known as the Sturmabteilung (SA). The SA imposed themselves on the streets of Munich, intimidating rival parties and symbolising Nazi anger.

Hitler's 1923 attempt to seize power, the Munich Putsch, was a spectacular failure. However, it was his trial for treason that gave him national coverage, during which Hitler took the opportunity to use his defence as an assault on the 'enemies' of Germany. The sympathetic judge sentenced him to five years in Landsberg Castle, of which he would only serve nine months and during which he dictated the infamous *Mein Kampf*.

Upon his release from prison Hitler found the party in chaos, with infighting and factionalism rife. This suited him. Able to cast himself as the saviour he re-established full control.

He then made a crucial decision. No longer would the Nazis attempt to seize power through violence or by coup. Hitler would now look to constitutional democracy as the route to influence and control. He would play its game and then shut down democracy from within.

However, 1925–9 were not good electoral years for the Nazis. As Germany basked in her international acceptance and the Golden Years seemed to gleam bright, who needed extremism? In 1928 the NSDAP made a terrible showing in the Reichstag elections, gaining a mere twelve seats. Although they had grown their support in rural areas, where agricultural depression had been a key issue for many, the urban areas gave Hitler very little support. However, the Wall Street Crash, and the Great Depression that followed, provided the perfect storm for Hitler and the Nazis to rise to the ascendency.

The major issue for Germany during the financial crisis was the aforementioned unemployment. This was so bad because of the reliance on foreign investment and a banking system built upon short-term loans. When investment was pulled out, the props were kicked from underneath Germany. Recovery was over. People were hurt, worried and angry. It was democracy itself that would take the brunt of this rage.

During the period 1930–32, warring parties in the Reichstag made effective government under Chancellor Brüning impossible. President Hindenburg intervened directly on an increasing number of occasions under Article 48 of the constitution. Parliamentary democracy was increasingly threatened.

At the same time as this, the Nazi Party grew exponentially in popularity. Hitler played upon the crisis, deploying effective propaganda, building influence and developing links with the traditional right-wing of German politics, the army and some rich industrialists. Hitler developed a very simple but alluring message: the Nazis promised work and bread and would eliminate the Bolshevik threat; anti-revolutionary, nationalistic and for the people. And it worked. In the 1930 Reichstag election the NSDAP became the second largest party with 107 seats.

In 1932, Hitler ran for President but failed to oust Hindenburg. However, in May, Brüning's government collapsed. Hindenburg first turned to the aristocrat Franz von Papen and then to General Schleicher to form a government – both failed. Then, finally,

The Führer – *Adolf Hitler.*

on 30 January 1933, Hindenburg appointed Adolf Hitler as Reich Chancellor. Hindenburg thought he could control the Nazi Party leader. He certainly thought that by exposing Hitler to the reality of the office, he would lose his air of mystique and the attraction that insurgent outsider politicians can hold.

Yet, within weeks the Weimar Republic would be taking its final breaths.

Two days after his appointment, Hitler called fresh elections to the Reichstag. Using a mixture of modern political campaigning, flooding the media with Nazi propaganda and taking his message directly to the people, along with the use of emergency powers to limit the activity of enemies of the state following the burning of the Reichstag (a murky affair seemingly carried out by one individual but tagged as a Communist/left-wing conspiracy by Hitler) the NSDAP – and centre-right parties in general – made considerable gains though did not gain a majority.

Following this triumph, emergency powers were used to expel all Communist Party members from the Reichstag and in March the Enabling Act was passed which, ultimately, gave the Chancellor the power to issue laws directly – thus neutering the Reichstag. By July, all parties apart from the NSDAP were shut down, with many simply giving up in their efforts to oppose Hitler. Hindenburg made no move to stop this as he had made his disgust at the parliamentary party system clear.

The Nazis gained great power in the regions by using SA gangs to instigate violent clashes and riots that forced individual states to turn to central government – the Nazis – for help, which they were only too happy to provide.

The final pieces fell into place when Hitler, showing his ruthless political brilliance, solved one of the crucial problems facing him: how could he guarantee the support of the Army? For some time, the SA had been increasing its power base and its leader, Ernst Röhm, had designs on subsuming the German Army under SA control and pressing on with more radical revolutionary change to Germany. The Army despised Röhm's SA and their uncouth street thug tactics. The Army could, with or without Hindenburg's approval, easily launch a *coup* against Hitler.

On Thursday, 12 April 1934, General Werner von Blomberg, German Minister of Defence, met Chancellor Hitler aboard the battleship *Deutschland*. It was here that a secret deal was struck whereby the Army would support Hitler in taking the Presidency upon the death of Hindenburg, in return for Blomberg retaining absolute control over military matters.

In July, Hitler unleashed a wave of violence and murder against many of those elements which he considered disruptive – including the leadership of the SA. This 'Night of the Long Knives' was useful in ridding Hitler of internal problems; but it also sent out the message that the most revolutionary elements of the movement were now under control. The Army had nothing to fear.

When Hindenburg died in August, Hitler moved quickly to combine the role of Chancellor and President and appoint himself *Führer* of Germany. The Army supported him, taking an oath of personal loyalty and allegiance.

Democracy was dead.

Hitler had complete political and military control of Germany.

The Third Reich was born.

> *'I swear before God to give my unconditional obedience to Adolf Hitler, Führer of the German Reich and of the German People, Supreme Commander of the Armed Forces, and will be ready as a brave soldier to risk my life at any time for this oath.'*
>
> the *Wehrmacht* (German Army) oath to Adolf Hitler

Steps to war

Upon taking charge of Germany's foreign policy in January 1933, Hitler initially moved cautiously. Germany, after all, was still regarded as a defeated state and France, in particular, harboured much mistrust of her. One of the main consequences of the Great Depression was the collapse of the reparations system and the failure of international disarmament – both key principles in the Versailles settlement. In October 1930 German representatives approached President Hoover of the USA and requested a moratorium on payments due to the current financial crisis. This Hoover Moratorium was granted; but it soon became evident that this was no brief economic downturn. At the Lausanne Conference (June 1932), Germany were relieved of ninety per cent of its outstanding debt. However, much to the chagrin of the USA, other European nations insisted that their war debts should also be heavily reduced. International co-operation was starting to fray.

The terms of the Treaty of Versailles had imposed major arms reductions on Germany. This was meant as the first step on the road to full international arms reduction. Hitler had always intended to revive German military power but, in these early years, he cut a rather isolated international figure and so acted with restraint until moments of opportunity presented themselves. An example of Hitler's diplomatic skill came at the Disarmament Conference (1932–33). The Weimar government, especially Gustav Stresemann, had shown a keen interest in a reduction of armaments across Europe. This was, it has to be said, not a solely humanitarian desire for world peace – any general reduction would undermine the limits placed upon Germany at Versailles. Although Hitler had little interest in following the principle of arms reduction, he could at least play along until it suited him.

The critical moment came when the French declined a British plan to reduce French and British troop numbers to 200,000 whilst allowing German numbers to rise to this level. Throwing up his hands in mock indignation towards a France who, he claimed, would never really support German reintegration into Europe, Hitler left the conference and, five days later, withdrew Germany from the League of Nations.

Hitler then pressed on…

By mid-1934, Hitler had increased the German Army to 240,000 men – more than double that permitted by Versailles and, furthermore, planned for an army of sixty-three divisions (roughly equal to that of 1914) by 1939. On 11 March 1935 he announced the official existence of the German *Luftwaffe*, once more breaching the treaty. A week later he introduced conscription and effectively tore up the military provisions of the peace settlement despite, only a month earlier, having told London's *Daily Mail* that 'Germany will of its own accord never break the peace'. This was a crucial moment; how would the rest of Europe react?

In moves reminiscent of the decades prior to the First World War, nations began scrambling for alliances. In April 1935, Britain, France and Italy formed the Stresa Front, whilst France signed a mutual assistance agreement with the Soviet Union. Italy, under Benito Mussolini and his fascist regime, was a crucial actor in the now turbulent seas of international diplomacy. At this stage, Mussolini was still distrustful of the young pretender in Berlin and his rise in both political and military power. *Il Duce* also had designs on extending Italian borders into Austria and had reacted to the assassination, by the Nazis, of the Austrian Chancellor Dollfuss in 1934 by sending troops to the Austrian frontier, in case Germany had attempted *Anschluss* at that moment. It would be some time before Mussolini would slide into the position of junior partner in the fascist firm.

Hitler continued to show his diplomatic prowess, particularly in negotiating bilateral agreements, such as the Anglo-German Naval Pact of June 1935. This limited the size of Germany's navy to 35 per cent that of the British; but it was far more significant in undermining the supposed solidarity of the Stresa Front. Although Hitler continued to wiggle and manoeuvre, it was apparent that he did not have the strength to take on all of Europe either politically or militarily. It was Italy's actions that would take Hitler from inside a claustrophobic diplomatic box and place him, instead, in a wide open field of expansionist possibilities.

In October 1935 Italian forces opened up an assault on the East African state of Abyssinia in both an attempt by Mussolini to fight 'war for war's sake, since Fascism needs the glory of victory' and to seek revenge for the humiliation of Italian forces at the hands of Abyssinian tribesmen at Adowa in 1896.

For Germany, this meant that Italy's attention was diverted from Austria. Britain and France now saw Italy as a hostile power and Britain applied economic sanctions against her. Furthermore, Britain's worries were focussed on Africa and the Mediterranean, where they thought that Mussolini might try to extend his influence further. This was a moment for Hitler to roll the dice.

On 7 March 1936, using only 22,000 troops and against the advice of his generals, Hitler took aim at the territorial clauses of the Treaty of Versailles: German soldiers marched into the Rhineland, a supposedly demilitarized zone. Surely this would trigger a response from the international community?

Due to French miscalculations over the size of the German force, British misgivings about confronting both Germany and Italy and a general malaise and weariness with commitments to Versailles, Hitler's gamble was a triumph.

From this moment on there was simply no hesitation by the *Führer*.

In October 1936 Italy and Germany agreed the Rome-Berlin Axis, a series of vague but symbolically important protocols, largely of an anti-Bolshevik nature. In November, Hitler sent the 'volunteer' Condor Legion of 12,000 men and *Luftwaffe* planes into action to support fascist General Franco in the Spanish Civil War. This was of particular importance to France, who now had another nationalistic and right-wing regime on her border. In November 1936, Germany and Japan formed the Anti-Comintern Pact against the Soviet Union, which Italy would join the next year. Meanwhile, Hitler had been reorientating the German economy onto a footing of self-sufficiency, or autarky, in preparation for war – something that would never actually come to be realised but that highlights the direction of travel that Germany was following.

In November 1937, Hitler called a top secret meeting at which he unveiled to his military inner circle the aims of his foreign policy – the rapid overthrow of Austria and Czechoslovakia followed by short wars against France and Britain, before turning to massive imperial expansion.[4] However, anyone who had read *Mein Kampf* would have been well aware of Hitler's dreams of a Greater Germany and *lebensraum* (living space) in the east. This meeting was so crucial because it significantly increased the pace of activity – so much so that, as soon as two fortuitous scandals gave him the opportunity, he moved swiftly to replace his War Minister (General Werner von Blomberg) and Commander-in-Chief of the Army (General Werner von Fritsch) because of their misgivings over his radical aims and rapid timeline for their completion.[5] By appointing no formal successor to Blomberg, Hitler in effect became Minister of War too, thus, helpfully, releasing him from his secret pact with Blomberg struck aboard the *Deutschland* four years previously. Hitler believed that he could hold a diplomatic and military advantage over France and Britain but that this would not last beyond the years 1943–5; therefore, he concluded, action with extreme violence at speed must be employed at once.

Completely violating the now worthless Versailles treaty, Hitler carried out *Anschluss* in March 1938 and brought Austria into the German Reich. The balance of power in Europe once again shifted: Germany had gained a border with Italy (who simply accepted *Anschluss*), threatened Czechoslovakia and secured routes to Hungary and the Balkans. Hitler was starting to believe himself an omnipotent power, whose instincts and military calculations were superior to those of his own cautious generals.

He next looked toward the Sudeten Germans, who had found themselves Czechoslovakian citizens following the redrawing of the map of Europe at Versailles.

The Czech crisis was complex, involving internal divisions within that country, as well as the most famous example of the policy of appeasement by British and French politicians. The Sudeten Czechs had for some time been agitating for autonomy within this fractious nation with several well-established ethnic groupings. Britain and France, understanding German intentions and concerned over troop movements in May 1938, began to put pressure on the Czechoslovakian government to concede to Sudeten demands or face the prospect of all-out war with Germany. Neville Chamberlain (British Prime Minister) and Edouard Daladier (French Prime Minister) entered into direct negotiations with Hitler, culminating in the Munich Conference of 29–30 September 1938. The outcome of this infamous *bête noire* was Chamberlain's declaration of an agreement between Herr Hitler and himself, stating that Germany and Britain would never go to war with one another again. Chamberlain, for a short period of time at least, was hailed as a hero in Britain. In return, Hitler had been given the green light for the gradual transfer of Czech territory where Germans were in a majority. In effect, Chamberlain had accepted the legitimacy of Hitler's goal of a Greater Germany and had set a dangerous precedent, at once raising the hopes of ethnic Germans in the east, who longed for a return to the Reich, and also encouraged the Nazis to carry on with this unification and expansion. The whole edifice of international security and collective strength had collapsed, especially evident when Hitler seized Prague in March 1939, thus proving the pact with the devil that was the Munich agreement.

Following the fall of Czechoslovakia, Britain and France finally stopped inhaling the opiate of appeasement, whose heady effects had lead them to believe they were the ones in control of the unfolding events in Europe. In reality, they had simply been handing out carrots and forgetting to bring their big stick.[6]

In March 1939, France and Britain issued a guarantee of Poland's borders. Hitler, now believing himself capable of outwitting all and dismissive of Anglo-French muscle-flexing, continued in his ambitious drive to unite and conquer. In May, Germany and Italy signed the Pact of Steel, which ultimately tied Italy militarily to Germany and vice-versa. In August the world gasped when Germany and the Soviet Union signed a Non-Aggression Pact.[7]

Using border incidents as a pretext for invasion, Hitler sent forces into Poland on 1 September. Much to his genuine surprise, Britain and France declared war upon Germany.

The twenty-year truce had come to an end.

Europe, and soon the world, was at war again.

> *'Close your hearts to pity. Act brutally.'*
> Hitler's words to his generals on
> the eve of the invasion of Poland.

'An inevitable war? Hitler's war? Appeasement to blame?': Historiography and the outbreak of the war.

Out of the rubble and smouldering ashes of war in 1945 came one very simple question for those who looked back and asked... 'why?' Why had this cataclysmic and devastating conflict been fought?

The immediate post-war analysis was that the First World War and the Treaty of Versailles left Europe in a precarious position – Germany was angry, bitter and broken. The Treaty was too harsh and future conflict inevitable. As soon as the world financial crisis created the necessary conditions, Adolf Hitler appealed to German resentment and started out on the journey of Germanic redemption. The utter failure of the policy of appeasement only encouraged the *Führer* further and, sure enough, the peace was shattered in 1939. As Winston Churchill put it, this was an 'unnecessary war'.

In 1961, the historian A.J.P. Taylor published his consensus-shattering *The Origins of the Second World War,* in which he argued that far too many people accepted the 'Nuremberg Thesis' without question: the belief that a small gang of extreme Nazis led by Hitler were to blame for the war. Instead he depicted Hitler as a normal human, one with abhorrent beliefs, but not an insane, evil, behemoth puppet-master. He pointed out that by laying the blame solely at the feet of Hitler, the rest of the German population and other world powers were being absolved of their responsibility. Taylor pointed out the similarities in German foreign policy since the time of Bismarck and argued that war broke out due to a series of mistakes and errors on the part of many statesmen in the decade before the war. He concluded that the war was not inevitable but that the destabilising Treaty of Versailles made it more likely than not and that Hitler took skilful advantage of the openings offered to him by the errors, caution and blundering of British,

French and Italian leaders. This work was radical and offended many but it re-opened the analysis of the causes and inevitability of the war and forever ended the simplistic notion that Hitler was to blame.

Although Taylor had forced historians to focus on other factors than the 'Hitler-did-it' thesis, many thought he was too blasé in his dismissal of *Mein Kampf* and the Hossbach Memorandum as no more than 'daydreaming, unrelated to what followed in real life'. Hugh Trevor-Roper argued vehemently that Hitler was not just a typical Western European politician playing diplomatic games and looking for openings; his analysis was that Hitler saw himself as some great force – a power in and of himself. His major conclusion was that Hitler was an intentionalist who had the conquest of Europe at the heart of his warped ideology. In the 1950s he had argued with Alan Bullock over the latter's analysis of Hitler as a 'mountebank' – an opportunistic adventurer with no fixed principles. Trevor-Roper also disagreed, therefore, with those who argued that Hitler was intent on world, rather than European, domination; this school of thought had its strongest advocacy in Andreas Hillgruber's numerous works, which highlighted Hitler as the important central force in a pre-planned global assault that would be carried out phase by phase.

A crucial outcome of A.J.P. Taylor's work was to point the finger at the pathetically weak actions of other nations, which gave Hitler the opportunities that he would exploit. Most notable was his evisceration of the policy of appeasement. Appeasement has today become a byword for cowardice, encouragement to aggressors and self-delusion. However, in the 1980s and 1990s British historian Richard Overy tried to bring some balance to this by pointing out that appeasement was only one part of Britain's global policy. He argued that Germany was a secondary concern to the British up until the mid to late 1930s. Britain was more concerned with Imperial Japanese threats in Asia, Mussolini's regime in Italy and Stalin's USSR. Moreover, Britain and France were still coming to terms with the deep economic shock of the Depression and, although ultimately a flawed policy, the need to appease was entirely understandable.

More recently, Gary Sheffield argued in the concluding chapter in his brilliant, iconoclastic work on the First World War, *Forgotten Victory* (2001), that when Taylor stated that Hitler was continuing classic German aims, and thus there was really a Thirty Years War from 1914–45 with a twenty-year pause in between, he was fundamentally mistaken. Sheffield points to the 1920s and highlights just how much of the Treaty of Versailles had been chipped away or completely revised and, therefore, to argue that the treaty had made further war inevitable was a nonsense. Hitler was *the* child of the Depression and if it were not for the Wall Street Crash then it is inconceivable to think of his rise to absolute power. Thus, although it is possible to think of a set of circumstances that would have led to conflict in Europe without Hitler, it would be highly unlikely to have had the same ferocity, with race-hatred at its core. The war, at least as it played out, was not inevitable.

Finally, Niall Ferguson carefully unpicked Neville Chamberlain's policy of appeasement in his 2006 book *War of the World*. His interesting conclusions on this policy paint Chamberlain in a rather different light. The Munich Agreement was, ultimately, a success for Chamberlain, in so far as he managed to outwit Hitler entirely and, through diplomatic brilliance, force him to abandon his plans to engulf Czechoslovakia immediately. However, this would be a short-lived triumph and, most tragically, Chamberlain had missed the opportunity to strike first. Ferguson makes the strong military, political and economic argument that had Britain declared war on Germany in 1938, perhaps standing up to them over *Anschluss*, then they would have likely won due to Germany's complete unpreparedness for war. Another year made a vast difference to the balance of power.[8]

For what it is worth, my own thoughts on the matter are that Hitler did not create a German foreign policy that was entirely new; but he did bring a ferocious racial and expansionist element that transformed the scope and ultimate ambition of the Reich that was intentional, took its lead from the *Führer* and can be supported by his thoughts in *Mein Kampf*, *Second Book* and *Table Talk*.[9] Hitler certainly planned war through many economic and domestic moves that can be seen within Germany in the mid-1930s, not least rearmament and the agenda advanced in the Hossbach Memorandum. He was also encouraged by the failure of Britain and France (appeasement policy) but this must be viewed through the wider lens of the crumbling of international co-operation created by the economic corruption of the Great Depression. It is true that firmer action was needed from Chamberlain and co. but this would have likely meant war earlier rather than no war at all.

Hitler certainly sought to expand the Reich in order to provide *lebensraum* in the east and to unite the German-speaking *völk*. Beyond these aims, however, we tread into the unknowable. Yet once he decided to act upon the opportunities that international diplomacy offered him in the late 1930s, any chance of a localised European conflict evaporated. Whether Hitler had aimed for a global conflict or not, one was about to erupt.

The War

1939

On 1 September 1939, Germany unleashed war with the invasion of Poland. On 3 September, France and Britain declared war on Germany. Over the next week, Australia, Canada, New Zealand and South Africa – as Commonwealth dominions – joined the British in military intervention against the Nazis.

By early October, Poland had been carved up between Germany and the Soviet Union and the 'Phoney War' – a period of limited combat but one of full military preparation – was under way. The USSR sent occupying forces into Estonia, Latvia and Lithuania and went to war (disastrously) with Finland over her rejection of territorial demands.

1940

In April Germany invaded Denmark and Norway, with the former falling within hours and the latter within two months. At the peak of the Norwegian crisis, Neville Chamberlain was replaced by Winston Churchill as Prime Minister on 10 May.

Also on 10 May, Germany launched assaults against France, Belgium, the Netherlands and Luxembourg. The German offensive took advantage of the Allies' mistaken belief that her forces would not be able to traverse through the Ardennes forest – they did and were able to trap Allied armies, threatening to encircle them and pushing them back towards the Channel. In early June, during the 'miracle' of Dunkirk, 300,000 mainly British and French soldiers were evacuated from the European mainland.

Italy invaded France on 10 June and also declared war on the United Kingdom. German forces occupied Paris by the 14th and eight days later France fully capitulated, signing an armistice with Germany. What would follow would be the division of France into German and Italian occupied zones plus an autonomous[10] Vichy Regime in the south.

Italy assaulted Malta in June, British Somaliland in August, part of Egypt in September and began a war with Greece in October. The latter descended into stalemate within days and Britain sent troops and air support to assist the Greeks.

In July the Battle of Britain began, with the German *Luftwaffe* attempting to incapacitate RAF Fighter Command. Hitler hoped to force the British to seek an armistice or, failing that, for German forces to prepare for the all-out amphibious and aerial invasion of Britain – *Unternehmen Seelöwe* (Operation Sea Lion). However, German strategy turned away from day-time raids in mid-September towards night-time assaults on industrial sites and cities (The Blitz). Although these attacks on civilian centres brought a sense of total war to the nation, it also hardened resolve. In mid-October, Hitler paused his plans for invasion and, by the end of the year, Operation Sea Lion was shelved.

In September, Japan, Italy and Germany agreed the mutual defence Tripartite Act, which would be strengthened by the addition of Hungary, Slovakia and Romania in November. In December, American President Franklin Roosevelt championed the passage of the Lend-Lease Act that sent aid to the British to support their war effort, whilst British and Dominion forces struck back against Italy in Africa.[11]

1941

In January the US and Britain began secret talks to determine plans for the defeat of Germany, should the USA enter the war.

In February German forces arrived in Africa to assist the Italians and within a month had driven the British forces back significantly.

Germany invaded and defeated both Yugoslavia and Greece in April, the same month that the Soviet-Japanese Neutrality Pact was signed.

On 22 June, Hitler broke the Non-Aggression Pact when Axis forces launched Operation Barbarossa – the invasion of the Soviet Union. Hitler's aim for the creation of *Lebensraum* in the East, the destruction of Communism and the annihilation of the Soviet military was under way. Germany also targeted the Ukraine region for its abundance of natural resources. In July the Soviet Union and Britain agreed a military alliance against Germany. The German assault had great initial success and by October all her objectives in Ukraine and the Baltic were achieved; but fighting still wore on in Leningrad. One of the initial aims of Barbarossa was the capture of Moscow within four months of the invasion. In August Hitler had paused on this objective whilst he diverted troops to Kiev; on 2 October, the attack began again. After two months of dreadful combat, in conditions plummeting well below freezing, the exhausted German forces suspended their offensive on 5 December. The *Wehrmacht* had unleashed an awesome *blitzkrieg* which had brought them to the gates of Moscow but, ultimately, they had failed to break Soviet resistance; from this stage onwards momentum slowed and German military omnipotence would be seriously questioned.

In August Britain and the USA issued an important policy statement, known as the Atlantic Charter. This agreement of post-war aims: self-determination; self-government; free-trade; freedom of navigation; freedom from want and fear; and disarmament of aggressors – was the basis for later co-operation and post-war planning.

On 7 December, the Empire of Japan launched near-simultaneous assaults on the Philippines, Thailand, Malaya, Hong Kong and the American Pacific Fleet stationed at Pearl Harbor. Although the specific attack at Pearl Harbor was a surprise, conflict had been likely for some time. In 1939 the USA had ripped up its trade treaty with Japan following the Japanese assault on China. Following an initial ban on aviation fuel, the Americans restricted trade in iron, steel and general mechanical parts when Japan invaded northern Indochina in 1940. It was these embargoes that forced Japan to make a decision between giving up her territorial ambitions in South East Asia and launching a war against Western forces. Britain and the Dutch government in exile, fearing Japanese incursions into their Asian possessions, began to prepare (alongside the USA) for joint defence in the area. A full oil embargo was also put into place. In late November negotiations between Japan and the USA broke down and thus the clock began to tick toward the 'day that will live in infamy'. Japan gambled that she could knock out the American Pacific fleet and then seize swathes of European colonies in Asia in order to create a perimeter defence. This would feed her need for resources and stretch the Allied military capacity to breaking point. Many talk of the madness of the Japanese attack on the Americans. However, looking at her aims and mind-set – Japan was never likely to simply give up her ambitions – such a move was logical, at least to the Japanese leadership.

Where madness did lie, however, was in Hitler's decision to declare war on the USA following Pearl Harbor. Citing the Tripartite Pact (Germany, Italy and Japan) and the fact that the USA had agreed a number of supportive moves with the UK, despite being technically neutral, Germany expanded the scale of her operations. Germany only had an obligation to defend Japan if she was attacked by a third party and, despite being counselled against the declaration, Hitler personally took the decision to insert Germany into the situation. John K. Galbraith, economist and advisor to President Roosevelt, summed up Hitler's actions thus: 'I cannot tell you our feelings of triumph. It was a totally irrational thing for him to do, and I think it saved Europe.' Galbraith was correct; it enabled Churchill to agree with FDR (and, in time, Stalin) a common approach to one global war rather than two separate, yet complex and intertwined, wars.

1942

This was a year for major Allied decision making. In January, twenty-six nations issued the 'Declaration by United Nations' which, in essence, committed them not to seek a separate peace with the Axis powers but to agree a collective strategy. It was also a wider agreement of the Atlantic Charter objectives. Throughout the year, the Allies analysed and debated strategic options. Understandably, the Soviets pushed for a second front to be opened up in Europe as soon as possible. The Americans initially had a preference for a mass armoured assault on Germany through France. However, it was the British vision that would be adopted. Persuading the USA that the Allies were not yet prepared for a major European landing, they argued that Germany should be worn down at the periphery, in areas such as North Africa, whilst simultaneously bombing Germany itself.

In early 1942 Germany rebuffed a major Soviet offensive in central and southern Russia before launching her own summer offensive in June. The aim was to capture the Azerbaijan oil fields in the Caucus region. Soviet forces positioned themselves to make a defensive stand against this assault on the River Volga, at Stalingrad. By November it looked as though the Germans would take the city; but then a Soviet counter-offensive began, which led to the encirclement of the German Sixth Army – comprising a quarter of a million troops.

On 19 August Allied forces carried out an assault on the German-occupied port of Dieppe, northern France. The aim was to seize the port for a short time, gather intelligence and to destroy fortifications, whilst proving to the Soviets the serious intent eventually to open up a second front. It was, in essence, a practice run for a future larger invasion. It was, however, an utter failure, with a sixty per cent casualty rate and very few objectives being achieved.

Throughout 1942 the Axis powers launched several offensives in North Africa, forcing the Allies into a deep retreat until they were able to halt them at El Alamein in Egypt; and then carry out a victorious counter-offensive in November. In the same month, Anglo-American landings (Operation Torch) in French North Africa forced Axis troops to withdraw to Tunisia. Hitler ordered an immediate occupation of Vichy France in response to French North Africa joining the Allies.

Throughout early 1942, Japan enjoyed a series of victories and had nearly achieved complete control over Burma, Malaya, the Dutch East Indies, the Philippines, Rabaul[12] and Singapore. In June the US won a decisive victory over the Imperial Japanese Navy at the Battle of Midway which proved to be a crucial turning point in the Pacific theatre. Allied forces then went on the offensive, notably in the Battle for Guadalcanal. The eventual defeat of Japanese forces in this battle in early 1943 marked the limit of Japanese conquest during the conflict.

1943

In January, at the Casablanca Conference, the Allies demanded the unconditional surrender of the Axis forces. This confirmed allied determination to annihilate the enemy. Invasion of Italy was also agreed upon.

Continuing to fight through appalling conditions, the surrounded German Sixth Army surrendered at Stalingrad on 2 February. Resulting in nearly two million casualties, it is considered to be one of the single deadliest battles of all time. The massive losses the Axis powers suffered (850,000) was a major blow and, many would argue, the turning point in the European theatre.

Throughout the year US, Canadian, New Zealand and Australian forces unleashed numerous operations against Japanese positions in the Pacific. In June the Combined Bomber Offensive (the strategic bombing of Germany by British and American air forces) began.

In July Germany attacked the Soviets at the Kursk Bulge but failed to achieve any success and the Soviet counter-offensive tipped the balance in its favour on the Eastern Front in general. In the same month, Allied forces invaded Sicily and the British firebombed Hamburg. By the end of July Mussolini had been removed from office and arrested.[13] In early September Allied forces were on the Italian mainland and began making their way northward towards the main German fortified position, the Gustav Line.

In November Winston Churchill and Roosevelt met with Joseph Stalin at the Tehran Conference. This meeting led to an agreement that a second front in Europe would be opened up in 1944 and that, once Germany was defeated, the Soviet Union would join the fight against Japan.

1944

The year began with a massive assault by the Allies against the Gustav Line, most notably at Monte Cassino, and with the beach landings at Anzio. On 27 January, after 872 days, Soviet forces drove German troops out of Leningrad, thus ending one of the longest and most appalling sieges in history.

By March Japan's Pacific perimeter had been breached and Rabaul was increasingly isolated. In the same month, Japanese forces attempted to invade India but, in a major turning point of the Burma campaign, British-led forces inflicted decisive defeats on the Japanese at Imphal and Kohima. In June the Japanese were defeated by US naval forces in the largest carrier-to-carrier naval battle in history, at the Battle of the Philippines Sea, and were defeated again at the Battle of Leyte Gulf in October.

By the early summer, Axis forces had been driven from the Ukraine and the Crimea and, in Italy, Rome was occupied by the Allies on 4 June. Later that month the Soviets launched the massive Operation Bagration, virtually annihilating German Army Group Centre and driving Axis forces from Belarus, followed by Western Ukraine, Poland[14] and Romania. Coups in Romania and Bulgaria brought these nations in to the Allied camp. Towards the end of the year, Axis forces were driven from Yugoslavia, Greece, Albania and Serbia, whilst Finland agreed an armistice with the USSR.

The much anticipated second front in Europe was opened up on 6 June with Operation Overlord. These Normandy landings were carried out, on the whole, by American, Canadian and British forces.[15] From here, the Allies began the process of pushing Germany back towards the Fatherland. Paris was liberated on 25 August. In September, the airborne Operation Market Garden was launched by the Allies, in and around the Dutch town of Arnhem, in an attempt to bypass German fortifications and secure important bridges over the Rhine and towns as a prelude to an invasion of north-west Germany. The operation failed and meant that the final stages of the war would be a slog, rather than a romp, to victory.

On 16 December Germany launched a major offensive through the Ardennes forest, with 400,000 troops. This caught the Allies off guard once again, with US forces soaking up the brunt of the onslaught. However, this 'Battle of the Bulge' was ultimately disastrous for the exhausted German forces and paved the way for the final Allied assaults and victory.

1945

By the end of January the Battle of the Bulge had ceased and a Soviet offensive had driven German forces from all of Poland. German-occupied Hungary fell to Soviet forces in February.

On 4 February Allied leaders met at the Yalta Conference and agreed on the terms of the post-war occupation of Germany and on the Soviet Union's entry into the war against Japan.

In the same month, Western Allied forces entered Germany and Soviet forces took Silesia. The following month, Western forces crossed the Rhine and encircled German Army Group B. On 12 April Roosevelt died and Harry S. Truman became US President. Soviet and Polish troops swept into Berlin that month and, on the 25th, American and Soviet soldiers linked up on the River Elbe.

Benito Mussolini was killed by Italian partisans on 28 April and the next day German forces surrendered in Italy. On April 30 Adolf Hitler committed suicide in his Berlin bunker. On 8 May Germany's total and unconditional surrender came into effect. The planned thousand-year Reich had lasted a mere twelve.

In south-east Asia, Allied forces recaptured Manila in March and made further major advances in the Philippines in April. 100,000 people were killed in Tokyo on 9/10 March by US incendiary bombing; over the coming months many more raids would be carried out all over Japan, killing as many as half a million civilians.

On 11 July Allied leaders (including new British PM Clement Attlee, replacing Churchill in mid-conference) met at Potsdam to confirm agreements regarding defeated Germany and again to demand the unconditional surrender of the Japanese.

In August the US dropped atomic bombs on the Japanese cities of Hiroshima and Nagasaki, whilst Soviet forces entered the fight against Japan. On 15 August Japan surrendered, with the official document signed on board the deck of the USS *Missouri* on 2 September.

The war was over.

* * *

Footnotes:

1. The First Reich was the medieval Holy Roman Empire of the German Nation, finally abolished in 1806; the Second Reich was created by Otto von Bismarck in 1871 and ended with the abdication of Kaiser Wilhelm II in November 1918.
2. US $468 billion or UK £306 billion equivalent in 2019.
3. Weimar Republic is the unofficial name for the German state from 1919–1933, taking its name from the city where its constitutional assembly first took place.
4. Fortuitously for history, this meeting was minuted by Colonel Friedrich Hossbach.
5. Blomberg resigned on 27 January 1938 when it emerged that his new wife had previously posed for pornographic photographs taken by a Czech Jew and that she also was listed on a Berlin police file as a known prostitute. Although almost certainly framed by Heinrich Himmler, Fritsch resigned after suspicion emerged that he was being blackmailed by a rent boy! Hitler would in due course remove another attendee at this meeting from his position: his Foreign Minister (Neurath).
6. By this stage at least Britain had begun a large expansion of what had become a dangerously underfunded and under-strength armed forces.
7. Hitler and Stalin stunned the world with this agreement. Whilst it seems that Stalin may genuinely have trusted the Pact, Hitler had played a masterstroke. Part of the agreement was for the Soviets to invade Poland in the east as Germany advanced in the west. Not only, therefore, did Hitler buy time before his invasion of the USSR but he created a common border

in order to make that advance easier. Stalin, for his part, had pushed Germany towards military adventure in Western Europe rather than to the east, or so he thought. The Soviet army was in no state at all to fight a major war due to the destruction of the senior ranks as a result of Stalin's so called 'Red Army Purges'.
8. Yet whether Britain had the military capability for this in 1938 is debateable. Also, the geopolitical realities of passing through other nations' territories to get to an aggressor nation is a conundrum that should never be overlooked i.e. if Britain had decided to act unilaterally in 1938, what would other European nations have done? Would they have joined them and/or allowed British forces across their borders?
9. *Mein Kampf* will be familiar to most but perhaps not the other two books. Hitler's *Second Book (Zweits Buch)* was unpublished during his lifetime but is now available in an unedited and translated format. It largely deals with his thoughts on foreign policy and expansion. Whereas *Mein Kampf* largely painted the Soviet Union as the ultimate enemy of the Nazis, Hitler shifts his emphasis towards the USA. He stressed the need for alliance with Britain in a European war and hypothesised about a decades-later clash between a conglomeration of European nations against the Jewish-plutocracy-dominated America. *Tischgespäche (Table Talk)* is a collection of Hitler's thoughts and remarks transcribed from 1941–44. The talks cover a range of topics from war to religion, personal ambition to culture.
10. Supposedly, but actually a German client-state.
11. The Lend-Lease Act supplied food, oil, weaponry, ships, planes and other vital items. Free France, the Republic of China and the USSR would also be recipients from this agreement.
12. A port town on the island of New Britain, Papua New Guinea. This would become a vital naval base for the Japanese during the war.
13. He would be rescued from prison by German paratroopers and 'ran' Italy from Lake Garda until his capture and execution in 1945. However, by that stage he was little more than a puppet ruler, under protection from his German liberators. Prime Minister Marshal Pietro Badoglio and King Victor Emmanuel were the ones actually ruling Italy; they negotiated the truce with the Allies and the declaration of war against the Nazis in October 1943.
14. On 1 August the Polish Resistance Home Army began its uprising against German occupying forces, timed to coincide with the Soviet advance. However, Red Army forces were deliberately held back and did not offer support. In Warsaw alone 200,000 civilians were massacred by German soldiers.
15. With further participation by Free French, Norwegian, Belgian, Danish, Dutch, Czech, Greek, Australian and New Zealand forces.

Remembrance, Memorialisation and the Commonwealth War Graves Commission

The Commonwealth War Graves Commission (CWGC)

In 1914, a forty-five-year-old director of an international mining company, finding he was too old to join the British Army, became commander of a mobile unit of the British Red Cross on the Western Front. This was Fabian Ware, a remarkable man and who is responsible for the beautiful cemeteries that you see today.

Ware had been deeply troubled in his first months in France by the obvious lack of an official recording process of the soldiers' graves, which were beginning to spring up near to the battlefields. Ware set about correcting this and, in 1915, his work with the Red Cross was officially recognized as one of great national importance, being transferred into a new Graves Registration Commission, part of the British Army. By the end of the year, agreement was reached with French authorities that land would be granted, in perpetuity, to the British Empire for the burial of the fallen and that the British would maintain the cemeteries.

By 1916 Kew Gardens were supplying seeds and plants for the cemeteries and on 2 May 1917 the body was granted a Royal Charter and named the Imperial War Graves Commission (IWGC). In the same year Ware began registering photographs of graves and graveyards for relatives of the dead.

Once the war ended, the real process of fully registering, recording and memorialising the dead could begin. It was immediately recognized that the importance of these cemeteries, as a symbol of sacrifice and as a place of pilgrimage, would be considerable.

At the outbreak of the Second World War, the Commission learned from the experience of the Great War and set about compiling information on the war dead and burials as well as earmarking land for use as cemeteries once the war ended.

At the end of the Second World War, the Commission had two major tasks: to return to tend for cemeteries and memorials of the Great War, sometimes rehabilitating them from destruction; and to set about creating new cemeteries for the dead from the most recent conflict. Fabian Ware was still Chairman of the organization during the Second World War but he was in the twilight of his years. He stepped down as Chairman in 1947 and fully retired from the Commission the following year, before dying in 1949 at the age of eighty.

'A corner of a foreign field' ... a CWGC cemetery.

As early as April 1946 all of the old Great War cemeteries were back under the watchful eye of the IWGC and in the same year work began on the new cemeteries. Initially working out of derelict buildings in the Normandy region, the IWGC completed the first five Normandy cemeteries before the end of 1950. The principal architect in Normandy was Philip Hepworth, whose style was very much in the tradition of Lutyens and Baker.[1]

The human cost of the war meant that 559 new cemeteries and 36 new memorials were constructed, with 350,000 new headstones erected. Extending its remit, at the request of Winston Churchill as recommended to him by Ware, the Commission created a roll of honour that commemorated 67,000 civilians who died as a result of the war.

In 1960 the commission was renamed the Commonwealth War Graves Commission (CWGC) and in 1964 its charter was extended to include the dead of the Second World War. Today the CWGC is responsible for the graves and memorials of 1.7 million Commonwealth service personnel. Of these, over one million rest in graves, with the others named on the various memorial walls. Its work spreads to 153 countries, with a full-time workforce of 1,200 people. This outstanding work ensures that those who lost their lives cannot be forgotten.

There are nineteen CWGC cemeteries in Normandy.

The cemeteries

After the Great War, amidst some heated parliamentary debate, two important principles were established for the cemeteries: first, bodies would not be repatriated due to the scale of the undertaking and the importance of the comrade-in-arms symbolism; secondly, the headstones would be uniform, so that no distinction would be made in rank or background.

Each headstone displays (if known) the number, rank and name, regiment, badge, age and date of death. An inscription, at a cost, could be chosen by the relatives[2] and the choice of a religious emblem was also permitted. Portland stone was the predominant material for the headstones of the Great War dead but Hopton Wood stone was used to a large extent following the Second World War; today Botticino stone from Italy is preferred, due to its durability. The headstones are 2ft 8in high, 1ft 3in wide and 3in deep.

The philosophy was to create tranquil, permanent resting places, with the feel of a British garden, which would inspire reflection and honour the dead.

After the death of his son at the Battle of Loos in 1915, Rudyard Kipling joined the Committee overseeing this work. Graves of soldiers whose remains could not be verified bear the inscription 'Known Unto God', which was selected by Kipling himself. He also suggested the verse from Ecclesiasticus, 'Their Name Liveth for Evermore', for inscription on the Stone of Remembrance, designed by Lutyens, which you will find in the larger cemeteries. In almost all of the burial grounds you will see the Blomfield-designed Cross of Sacrifice – the only clearly Christian symbolism, which even then is modified by the fact that it fits the sword hilt, part of the design.

Nearly all of the cemeteries have a small bronze box set in, usually, a cemetery wall that reveals a recess which contains within the cemetery register and a visitors' book. Please do sign the latter and encourage your students and/or fellow visitors to do the same.

Memorials

In the instances where bodies were not found their names are commemorated on a series of impressive memorials across France and Belgium. For example, the Bayeux memorial bears the names of more than 1,800 men of the Commonwealth land forces who died during the Normandy campaign and have no known grave.

Visiting a particular grave or memorial panel

If you are wishing to visit the grave of a relative, or locate them on a memorial, then make use of the brilliant website, www.cwgc.org, where you can start your search on the home page. If you have a name, the website will provide you with the cemetery and the plot and row where the grave can be located. For memorial panels, you will be given the panel number. If you do not have full details, or if – as can happen – the official record seems to be incorrect, then contact the CWGC: they will do all that they can to help you. One other important point: it is a good idea to take a copy of the layout of the cemetery with you in order to help locate the plot once you arrive. This can be gained from the website too. A copy should be in with the register details at the cemetery, but they can go missing.

The American Battle Monuments Commission (ABMC)

The ABMC was set up in 1923 and has the task of maintaining and running the US military cemeteries, monuments and memorials both in the USA and abroad. The President appoints the Chairman of whom there have been some highly notable incumbents such as General John J. 'Black Jack' Pershing (1923–48) and General George C. Marshall (1948–59). The ABMC looks after fifty-two sites that cover both World Wars and also those relating to the Mexican-American War, the Spanish-American War, the Korean War, Philippine-American War and US Civil War. There are 124,905 US servicemen and servicewomen interred at these sites and over 94,000 missing in action, or lost or buried at sea, whose names are recorded on the monuments.

The Normandy American Cemetery and Memorial.

Much like the CWGC cemeteries, US cemeteries in France are on land granted free and in perpetuity by the French State. They are also astonishingly well-kept and a fitting memorial to the fallen. American cemeteries certainly bring a sense of grandeur and power – they remind one of Washington D.C. itself, with the gleaming stonework, neo-classical designs and sheer scale. The cemeteries contain visitor books, a non-denominational chapel, battle map displays and various sculptures. The headstones are white marble crosses, except for those of the Jewish faith, who have a tapered design with a Star of David atop. For those who are buried but whose names are unknown, the inscription reads: 'Here Rests in Honored Glory a Comrade in Arms Known but to God'.

However, it is important to note that, unlike those killed in the World Wars from Britain and her Commonwealth and Dominions, all US servicemen had the right to be repatriated for burial at home, either in National Cemeteries (such as the magnificent Arlington, Virginia) or in a private/family plot closer to their home.

There are two American Cemeteries in Normandy, the most famous of which is the Normandy American Cemetery and Memorial on bluffs above Omaha Beach.

The Commission has a searchable database on its website; if you are wishing to locate a particular burial or memorial then visit https://www.abmc.gov/.

German War Graves Commission (Volksbund Deutsche Kriegsgräberfürsorge)

The Commission is responsible for the upkeep of German war graves in Europe and North Africa and is similar in operation to the CWGC and ABMC. It was founded in 1919 as a provision of the Treaty of Versailles and had established many cemeteries by the 1930s in order to bury their Great War dead. However, given the events of 1939–1945, work halted and it was not until 1956 that the organization continued with its work of burying the dead of the Great War and beginning the process of burying those of the Second World War. The Commission currently takes care of 832 war cemeteries and graves in forty-five countries, the final resting places for 2.7 million war casualties.

There are far fewer German cemeteries of both World Wars than for those of the Allies. They also tend to be concentration burial sites on smaller plots, given post-war feelings towards the aggressor nation from the nations whose land they invaded. German soldiers could be repatriated but an astonishingly high number are unaccounted for. However, since the end of the Cold War the Commission has undertaken a mass investigation into the resting places of missing soldiers, particularly in Eastern Europe, where the majority of the missing are likely to be, but also in the west too. There were an extraordinary 36,943 exhumations in the year 2013 alone.

Unlike its American and British counterparts, the German Commission is voluntary and relies on gifts and donations to further its work. During the summer months you will likely see international school children looking after the graves and cemeteries. They volunteer during their school holidays to undertake this role.

You will find a searchable database at www.volksbund.de.

* * *

Footnotes:

1. The three main architects tasked with designing and realizing the Cemeteries and memorials of the First World War in France and Belgium were Sir Edwin Lutyens, Sir Herbert Baker and Sir Reginald Blomfield. The planting schemes were designed by Gertrude Jekyll.
2. The New Zealand authorities did not grant this option.

D-Day: A Glossary of some Key Terms

Allied Expeditionary Force (AEF): see **SHAEF**

Atlantic Wall: the German chain of fortifications which stretched along the coastline between Norway and the French border with Spain.

Belgian Gate: A metal structure which would be hidden by high tides. Part of the Atlantic Wall defences, it was designed to rip the bottom out of any landing craft.

Bigot: Security clearance term for those with knowledge about Overlord. Hence, you were 'bigoted' if you were in the know!

Bocage: The thick hedgerows in the Normandy countryside. The Allies were slowed down in the days following D-Day by fighting in such tricky terrain.

BODYGUARD (Operation Bodyguard): General name for the deception plans for Allied operations in Europe.

BOLERO (Operation Bolero): Codename for the build-up of US forces in Britain in preparation for Overlord.

D-Day: Military term to denote the day on which an exercise or operation will begin. This is a standard term, still in use today. D+5 would refer to five days after the initial operation began. It was and is helpful to use this term when planning, rather than the actual dates, as it means the date can change without having to update written material, for example.

DUKW: An amphibious truck used to deliver supplies from ships to shore.

Eisenhower, Dwight D.: Supreme Commander of the Allied Expeditionary Force on D-Day.

Funnies (Hobart's Funnies): Major General Percy Hobart worked on a number of modifications and inventions which were used during Overlord. His fleet of tanks which had various special roles (e.g. mine clearance, ditch crossing, floating, flame-throwing) were hugely successful, especially on British landing beaches. One critique of American landing forces was their decision not to utilize these to the fullest extent.

FUSAG: First United States Army Group – a completely fictitious Allied Army Group. Based in Kent, it was created to deceive the Germans over where the Allies would land in France. US General George S. Patton was placed in command of this phantom force as Hitler believed him to be America's finest general, who was likely to command any invasion.

A beautiful Mulberry Harbour vista.

FORTITUDE (Operation Fortitude): The deception plan conceived to mislead Germany about where the invasion would take place.

Gold (Gold Beach): British landing zone between Le Hamel and Ver-sur-Mer.

Gooseberries: Artificial harbours created by sinking Allied ships in order to create breakwaters.

H-Hour: Standard military term referencing the hour at which an exercise or operation will begin. As with D-Day, H-Hour+3 would denote three hours after the operation began. H-Hour-1 would be the hour before it began.

Hedgehog/Czech Hedgehog: Beach obstacles hidden by high tides and made of three metal beams welded together. Part of the defence system of the Atlantic Wall.

Juno (Juno Beach): Canadian landing zone from Courseulles-sur-Mer, east of Gold Beach, to Saint-Aubin-sur-Mer, west of Sword Beach.

LCA: Landing craft, assault

LCI: Landing craft, infantry

LCT: Landing craft, tank

LCVP: Landing craft, vehicle and personnel – known as the Higgins Boat. Could carry up to thirty-six men. Generally acknowledged as being vital to the success of the Normandy landings.

Mulberries: Artificial portable harbours that were towed across the Channel and positioned near Omaha and Gold beaches on D-Day. A storm later destroyed the Omaha harbour.

Nazi: (largely) derogatory term for the National Socialist German Workers Party (NSDAP).

NEPTUNE (Operation Neptune): The code name for the naval operations in support of Overlord.

Omaha (Omaha Beach): American landing zone from the east of Sainte-Honorine-des-Pertes to the west of Vierville-sur-Mer.

OVERLORD (Operation Overlord): Code name for the D-Day invasion, 6 June 1944.

Panzer: German main battle tanks.

Piat: A portable anti-tank weapon.

Piccadily Circus: codename given to the area of the English Channel that served as the rendezvous point for the vessels taking part in Operation Neptune.

PLUTO (Pipeline Under the Ocean): Pipelines were laid across the channel and fuel pumped across from pumping stations in England to fuel the Allied invasion.

Rommel's Asparagus: Part of the German defence against Allied gliders and paratroopers. Consisting of wooden logs 4–5 metres in height and placed in fields and meadows in Normandy.

A gun emplacement at the Longues Battery.

Rupert: Nickname for the parachute dummies, three feet tall and made from cloth bags stuffed with sand and straw, dropped by the Allies to confuse the German forces. Approximately 500 were dropped around Normandy, away from the real drop zones – they proved quite effective at confusing the German response on the ground. Rupert was also a British Army nickname for young officers.

SHAEF: Supreme Headquarters Allied Expeditionary Force. The Allied force under the command of General Dwight D. Eisenhower. The following countries supplied troops to the AEF: Australia, Belgium, Canada, Czechoslovakia, Free France, Netherlands, New Zealand, Norway, Poland, Great Britain and the United States of America.

Sword: British landing zone from Ouistreham to Saint-Aubin-sur-Mer. It was the eastern most landing beach of the invasion.

Teller Mine: German antitank mine. Waterproof versions were formidable obstacles for landing craft on the Normandy beaches.

Tetrahedron: Another obstacle used by the Germans to sink landing craft.

TONGA (Operation Tonga): Airborne operation undertaken by the British 6th Airborne Division during the night of 5–6 June. Objectives: to capture and then hold the bridges over the Caen Canal and Orne River (*coup-de-main*); destroy the German artillery battery at Merville; to secure the areas between the Orne and River Dives.

Ultra: The designation for the intelligence data gathered from the interception and decryption of German 'Enigma' communications.

Utah (Utah Beach): American landing zone located between the villages of Pouppeville and La Madeleine. The westernmost landing beach.

Normandy and D-Day: A History

Normandy

Humans have inhabited the area now known as Normandy since pre-historic times. The Gauls settled the lands from the fourth century BC until Julius Caesar's conquest in 51 BC. The Romans remained in control until a period of instability, commencing in the late third and early fourth century, due to a series of Germanic and Saxon raids; Christianisation occurred during the early Middle Ages. However, it was in the ninth century that the Scandinavian invasions and colonisation of the region took place and from where we derive the name Normandy – 'men of the north'.

From 911, the Viking leader Rollo became the first ruler of Normandy and his successors gained the title of the Duke of Normandy. The most famous of these was William I – the Conqueror – who spread Norman influence and power, not least with the invasion and conquest of England in 1066. Although these rulers accepted the overlordship of the King of France, they were practically the head of an independent region.

French Normandy was occupied by English forces for long periods of the 100 Years' War (1337–1453) and was blighted again by conflict during the French Wars of Religion (1562–98). However, after this, the area settled into an era of peace and prosperity, largely managing to avoid the tribulations of the French Revolution (1789–99), the Napoleonic Wars (1803–15), the Franco-Prussian War (1870–71) and the Great War (1914–18).[1] The province blossomed and became a coastal tourism hot-spot. With its beautiful rolling green fields, sandy beaches, ancient castles, stunning architecture and, of course, fabulous gastronomic delights,[2] Normandy bathed in its own beauty and ebullient pleasures… that is, until the Fall of France in 1940.

France under occupation

Following her defeat, the French Third Republic came to an inglorious end and was replaced by the French State – more commonly known as Vichy France, from the name of the spa town in which the government was seated. Although nominally in charge of all of France, this was little more than a puppet authority headed by the Great War hero, Marshal Philippe Pétain. Much of the north and west of France was ruled directly by a German Military Administration. This was extended further when, in November 1942, following the Allied landings in North Africa, the Military Administration implemented direct rule across Vichy France as well. The German Reich was, in reality, the occupying power, with Pétain's Government the facilitators of Nazi directives.

44 *Visiting the Normandy Invasion Beaches and Battlefields*

Fascist paramilitary organisations, such as the *Milice Française*, created by the Vichy regime used torture and assassination whilst assisting with the rounding up of Jews for deportation. This is an extreme example of the extent of French collaboration. However, at the other end of the spectrum, on the eve of D-Day there were approximately 100,000 French Resistance fighters actively working to undermine the Nazi occupation. Tens of thousands more joined the Resistance once the liberation was under way.

In Normandy itself life under the occupation was a relatively calm one, with many choosing a quiet life – happy to trade their wares and co-exist with the German troops stationed there.

Festung Europa – Fortress Europe

In December 1941, following the Japanese attack on Pearl Harbor and the subsequent US entry into the war, Adolf Hitler instructed his military command to plan and then build a series of defensive positions to protect the Arctic, North Sea and Atlantic coast lines against possible invasion. This would become known as the Atlantic Wall – the 'impenetrable' defensive line of Hitler's Fortress Europe.

The system consisted of bunkers, pillboxes, gun emplacements and concrete strongpoints and used 13.2 million cubic metres of concrete and 1.3 million tonnes of steel in its construction. The work was carried out by a mixture of French forced labour, Russian and Polish prisoners of war and was overseen by the German construction engineer Fritz Todt.

In 1940 there were Allied raids on the French coast; in March 1941 a commando assault on the Lofoten islands; February 1942 saw paratroopers dropped into the German radio-location site at Bruneval, close to Le Havre. The Allies were preparing, practising, planning; Hitler was well aware that an invasion attempt would come, of this there was no doubt. However, if it could be thrown back into the sea then he felt it would drive an irreconcilable wedge between the Allies, perhaps encouraging Stalin to break free from the uneasy alliance.

On 23 March 1942, Adolf Hitler issued his *Führer* Directive Number 40:

> 'The coastline of Europe will, in the coming months, be exposed to the danger of the enemy landing in force [...] Enemy forces that have landed must be destroyed or thrown back into the sea by immediate counterattack.'

Five days later, the *Normandie* dry dock at St Nazaire was attacked in a successful British amphibious assault. Operation Chariot targeted St Nazaire because the loss of its vast dry dock would require large German warships to return to Germany for repairs, thus exposing them to attack by the Royal Navy.

Then, in August, a disastrous Allied amphibious assault on Dieppe was launched, culminating in a sixty per cent casualty rate amongst the largely Canadian infantry forces, who were outmanned, exposed, insufficiently supported by naval and aerial power and fighting against a position already on high alert of a likely assault. The aim had been to secure experience in making an opposed landing on coastal positions – a jab at the chin of Fortress Europe. What happened was a mauling of the Allies... but many important lessons were learned. Allied Commander Lord Mountbatten said, years after the war: 'I have no doubt that the Battle of Normandy was won on the beaches of Dieppe. For every man who died in Dieppe, at least ten more must have been spared in Normandy in 1944.'

Although German propaganda made much of the Allied disaster at Dieppe, Hitler knew that the Allies would be back and he redoubled efforts to increase the size and scope of the Atlantic Wall.

When and where this attack would take place was the great unknown for the German high command. With approximately 3,000 miles of coast line to defend, this left a number of possible locations for the Allied landings. Many believed that the most likely target would be somewhere in the Pas de Calais area, given that this was the shortest route for a Channel crossing. However, they also considered that the Allies might try a feint attack in one area before hitting the real zone.

The man charged with the command of Fortress Europe was the sixty-nine year old aristocrat, Field Marshal Gerd von Rundstedt. Prior to the war he had been in retirement but, dragged back into service, he had already proven himself during the invasion of France and his command of forces on the Eastern Front. He was a confident, strong-willed man, who had never lost a battle. He was also quite willing to stand up to the *Führer* – indeed he was made Commander in Chief of Army Group West in 1942 after his removal from the Eastern theatre due to criticisms he made of Hitler's strategy there.

Field Marshal Gerd von Rundstedt.

It was the continuing drain of manpower and resources in the East throughout 1943 that led von Rundstedt to report in October that, given the shortage of mines, weapons, quality troops and obstacles, the wall could be covered but not properly defended. In response, Hitler wasted little time in issuing *Führer* Directive Number 51, which stated that 'I can no longer justify the further weakening of the West in favour of other theatres of war. I have therefore decided to strengthen the defences in the West.' Two days later, 'The Desert Fox', Field Marshal Erwin Rommel, was appointed as Inspector General of Defences in the West. Rommel acted with great dynamism, carrying out a full and exhaustive review of the Wall from Denmark to the Spanish border. The outcome was a highly critical report that led to Rommel's Army Group B being incorporated into von Rundstedt's Army Group West, with Rommel under von Rundstedt's command, yet having specific responsibility for anti-invasion planning.

Rommel ordered the laying of millions of mines, a mass barbed wire reinforcement, multiple beach defences and for fields to be spiked with 'Rommel's Asparagus' anti-glider poles. This huge increase in defensive work was not unnoticed by Allied reconnaissance, as a result of which the invasion plans were switched from a night time to a dawn assault, in order that troops would be better able to traverse the myriad of beach obstacles.

Rommel's arrival and incorporation into the Army West's command structure further complicated an already confusing decision-making system: this played out most notably

Rommel and the Führer.

General Guderian.

over how best to deploy the armoured panzer forces. Rommel was convinced that the only way to stop an invasion was as it occurred, on the beaches and in the first forty-eight hours. Do not allow any foothold on Fortress Europe.

Therefore, he demanded control of the nine armoured divisions in Panzer Group West, so that he had the fluidity and flexibility to deploy them where required as soon as the invasion began. In order to do this at speed successfully, the divisions would have to be kept close to the coastline, concentrated in areas near to the likely invasion sites. And it was here that the German high command mired itself in internecine war with that classic military clash of cultures: caution versus aggression.

General Guderian (Inspector General of Panzers), supported by the veteran Panzer commander General Geyr von Schweppenburg (responsible for training the Panzer divisions under von Rundstedt), worried about the exposure of these vital formations to Allied air power under such a plan and preferred holding the divisions further back until the intentions of the invasion became clear – then a mass counter attack could be launched. Von Rundstedt, crucially, favoured this more traditional, cavalry style, textbook assault. Given the supremacy of Allied air power, his desire to hold these crucial resources away from the immediacy of the front line is entirely understandable.

Hitler, although sympathetic to Rommel, compromised. Three of the nine Panzer divisions were handed to Rommel and the rest remained with von Rundstedt – although they could only be released by direct authority from the *Führer* himself! Rommel, one of the greatest tank commanders in history, who had learned during the North Africa campaign of the necessity to maintain one's reserves well forward, was overruled. It is on such decisions as this that the future of nations can hang.

To complicate matters even further, the Navy and Air Force operated independently of von Rundstedt and, therefore, when the invasion came, the morass of command centres created chaos during the dense fog of war.

On D-Day Rommel had thirty-nine infantry divisions alongside his three Panzer divisions. The closest Panzer division was near Caen, with the other two near to Paris and Amiens respectively.

Who were these soldiers, tasked with the vital defence of Fortress Europe and on whom the future of the Third Reich itself would hang?

In theory, von Rundstedt had command of close to 1.5 million men of the *Wehrmacht* in Army West. However, the general quality of these troops was poor. By 1944 German troops in the West were not those envisioned when Hitler had said he would create an army 'the likes of which the world had not seen'. Old or desperately young men, 'ear and stomach battalions'[3] and conscripts from Alsace, Lorraine and Luxembourg were common place. In the Normandy sector, there were some 50,000 *Wehrmacht* troops of the Seventh Army but, astonishingly, a fifth of these were Polish or *Osttruppen* – eastern troops recruited from the occupied territories and Soviet prisoners of war. Some had volunteered in an attempt to survive the war, but many were conscripts with no choice in the matter. Hence, German officers doubted their loyalty and they were correct to do so – many *Osttruppen* did surrender to the Allies (or turned around and shot their German superiors) once D-Day began.[4]

Indeed, it is fair to conclude that, in Normandy, this was no advertisement for the self-proclaimed Aryan master race super-force.

When summarizing the problems facing Nazi Germany in 1944, the most basic one was the most crippling: she occupied more land than she could defend. Initially, of course, Hitler had learned the lessons of the First World War – Germany could not win a war of attrition on a mass scale against multiple foes. The *blitzkrieg* successes of 1940–41 seemed to herald this new military dawn. Yet, once the Nazi war machine began to freeze to death on the Eastern Front, Hitler's inflexibility – his unyielding desire to defend every inch of land captured – only made the situation for his armed forces worse.

Von Rundstedt himself fully understood the fallibility of the Atlantic Wall. This supposed bulwark; the critical defensive line; the Nazi spectacle of strength and might was, he acknowledged, 'a myth, nothing in front of it, nothing behind – a mere showpiece'.

That is the problem with defensive lines – once you break through them, what is left?

Frederick the Great once said that 'he who defends everything defends nothing.' Hitler should have heeded the advice of one of his Prussian heroes far more carefully than he did. The *Führer* truly seemed to believe that Fortress Europe would hold – it would be defended to the last man, the aggressors would be hurled back into the sea.

The truth was that this unfinished, highly vulnerable and poorly manned system was a paper tiger in which very few senior commanders, beyond the fundamentally flawed *Führer* himself, believed.

Planning

The plan for the Allied assault on the Normandy coast line was codenamed Overlord. Following the removal of Axis forces from North Africa and the establishment of an Allied foothold in Italy, Generals Eisenhower and Montgomery were recalled to London to prepare for the invasion of Western Europe. Eisenhower was given the position of Supreme Commander whilst Montgomery would lead the land forces.

In some ways they were an odd couple: Monty, in his usual terse and derogatory way, commented on Eisenhower after the war that he was a 'nice chap, no soldier'. He had also famously admonished Eisenhower for smoking in his presence during their first meeting. However, unlike Eisenhower's deputy, Air Chief Marshal Sir Arthur Tedder, who loathed Montgomery, Eisenhower had a sunny ambivalence that enabled him to rise above petty politics and, more importantly, made him the ideal man to keep a quite disparate command structure together. Winston Churchill had little time for Tedder; General Omar Bradley, a man from a poor Missouri farming background and who still managed to look as such, was about the most opposite one could be as a person to the God-fearing, larger than life, foul-mouthed, self-aggrandizing, wild-card that was General George Patton. Air Chief Marshal Leigh-Mallory, a man who always seemed to spread doubt about operations with his doom-laced, last-minute concerns, managed to annoy almost everyone. This was not an easy team to manage.

General Omar Bradley.

Eisenhower did a remarkable job: just before D-Day he was a chain-smoking nervous wreck whilst he contemplated the weight of the task upon him, but to those around him he still radiated the air of the light-hearted, laid-back, favourite uncle, who spread calm simply by his very presence and steady certainty.

The planning for the invasion had begun as early as 1941 under the codename Roundup. A later plan, Sledgehammer, considered an invasion in the Pas de Calais and General George C. Marshall, the US Army Chief of Staff, had drawn up his own plan for an assault over infamous ground, blood-soaked by a previous generation: the Somme.

Political considerations were interwoven with military realities. In general, President Roosevelt favoured a dual assault on France – both north and south instantaneously – to

Eisenhower, Leigh-Mallory, Tedder and Montgomery.

be carried out as soon as possible. Churchill favoured an assault in the Mediterranean, drawing German forces into Italy, whilst the Soviets wore them down in the East, before a single invasion point, sometime in 1944, in France. Much has been written on this subject but, although Churchill's reticence to launch the assault in the West too early now seems well judged, FDR had to walk a tightrope of US public opinion (and many of the views of his own staff and commanders too) who felt that the British were simply far too cautious. We have to remember that Roosevelt had agreed a Germany-first strategy in order to support Churchill – the President could always change course and send his forces to the Pacific front. During the Casablanca Conference in January 1943 the Allies agreed to establish a planning organisation that would prepare for the invasion.

Lieutenant General Sir Frederick Morgan, as Chief of Staff to the Supreme Allied Commander (at that point a position not yet filled), led the team that drew up these plans in 1943, drawing on the work of Roundup, Sledgehammer et al. This group was known as COSSAC. Their plans envisaged an assault on Normandy, the capture of ports, consolidation and then an inland advance. It was decided that some kind of artificial harbours would be required and that fuel would be delivered by a Pipeline Under the Ocean (PLUTO); Lord Mountbatten as Chief of

Lieutenant General Morgan.

Combined Operations would lead on these aspects. 1 May 1944 was the date pencilled in for the assault. At the Quebec Conference in August 1943, these plans were accepted by the Allied military leadership.

COSSAC morphed into SHAEF (Supreme Headquarters Allied Expeditionary Force) and Eisenhower based its HQ at Bushey Park, Richmond upon Thames.

In January 1944 Montgomery was briefed on the initial plan that had been developed the previous year, 'Monty' accepted the overall thrust but was far from impressed with some of the detail. In essence, he removed the part of the operations that focused on attacking Caen itself, increased landing forces to the strength of five divisions and airborne divisions to three, thus stretching the Germans in any counter attack, and widened the designated assault area to fifty miles of coastline. Protecting the flanks of the assault beaches would be key and this was the main reason for the increase in airborne numbers.

At this time D-Day was delayed until 31 May 1944.

Lord Mountbatten.

The land operation would be divided into two sections: to the West was the First US Army under General Bradley and to the east the Second British Army under General Miles Dempsey. The American beaches carried the codenames Utah and Omaha and the British and Canadian sectors were Gold, Juno and Sword. The American airborne divisions would drop at the far west and the British at the far eastern point. Furthermore, following a successful landing phase, the aim was for the Americans to break out west, capture Cherbourg and advance into Brittany. The British and Canadians would tie down German forces before breaking out and linking up with US forces later on.

Successful leaders are judged on the decisions that they make: Eisenhower had many crucial ones to consider. He would have the final say on the actual date of D-Day, made even more onerous by the number of considerations to take into account. Tactical surprise is always vital on a battlefield and, to that end, it is no shock that those heading the landing phase wanted to go in to combat during the hours of darkness. However, naval and air forces preferred daylight conditions so that accurate bombing was more likely to be assured.

Given Rommel's huge expansion of beach defences, it was deemed important for troops to be able to see them in order to traverse them. Therefore it was agreed that the time of the attack should be approximately three hours before high tide and ten minutes after sunrise.

General Miles Dempsey.

In order that airborne divisions could be dropped and gliders locate their landing zones with accuracy, good moonlight was essential. What did all this mean for Eisenhower?

He was warned that he only had three days per month when conditions would meet these requirements. And that was if the weather was good…

Throughout 1943 and into 1944, southern England began to build up into one vast army camp, ready to deploy across the channel in the largest amphibious assault seen in the history of the world. Yet this most ambitious of undertakings would have been destroyed if it had to assault the bulk of the *Wehrmacht* in the West.

The Allies had to make German High Command look away first…

Deception

> 'If the enemy obtains as much as forty-eight hours' warning of the location of the assault area, the chances of success are small, and any longer warning spells certain defeat.'
>
> COSSAC

> Churchill: 'In wartime, truth is so precious that he should always be attended by a bodyguard of lies.'
> Stalin: 'This is what we call military cunning.'
>
> *Conversation during the Tehran Conference,
28 November–1 December 1943.*

Once the huge amphibious invasion force began to assemble, it was clearly impossible to fully hide it from German observation. Therefore, on 6 December 1943, John Bevan of the London Controlling Section[5] began preparations for the deception plans for Overlord. This operation, with a nod to Churchill's shrewd phrase, was called Bodyguard. First, the planning aimed to force Hitler and his staff to believe that the invasion could come in several possible areas and thus affect the positioning of German forces throughout Europe. Secondly, the operational aim was to mislead them as to exactly which location and with what strength the assault would be launched.

There were several strands and sub-operations to Bodyguard:

Fortitude North deception: an invasion of Norway, using the phantom British Fourth Army

Fortitude South deception: an invasion of the French Pas de Calais region by the fictional First United States Army Group (FUSAG)

It was vital that the above two plans were successful. Montgomery knew that he had to have some time to turn the initial landing into a secure beachhead and then a strong footing on mainland Europe. In order to do this the Germans had to be convinced, even once the invasion was under way, that it was merely a diversionary attack, thus giving crucial time to the Allies whilst Hitler held back his reinforcements. The British Fourth Army was supposedly headquartered in Edinburgh Castle. FUSAG was stationed at

General George S. Patton – commander of the phantom FUSAG.

Dover under the command of Patton and this, arguably, was the most successful aspect of the deception plans. Pas de Calais was the most logical invasion site, given that it is the shortest crossing route from England, and that Hitler and Rommel held Patton in high regard, the Germans fell fully for this aspect of Bodyguard – so much so that six weeks after the Neptune landings in Normandy, Hitler had still not sent his reinforcements from the Pas de Calais.

Why had the FUSAG smoke and mirrors operation worked so well?

The location of this 'Army' and Patton's notional command were of course vital. But there were many more crucial elements in addition. Since April 1944, false radio communications – including recordings of battlefield training operations – and Morse code signals were pumped out for the benefit of German wireless-eavesdropping. Not only were fake tanks and landing crafts constructed but they were 'serviced' by real crews. At night, Dover and the surrounding areas were a hive of 'activity', with lighting used to simulate movement. King George VI even inspected a (fake) oil terminal, a visit reported in the press for the consumption of German intelligence operatives.

Crucially, all of this worked, not least because of the work of MI5 double agents, such as Juan Pujol Garcia (GARBO), who fed corroborating 'evidence' directly to his handlers. On the eve of D-Day it was a widely held belief amongst senior Nazi officials and Army commanders that the majority of Allied forces were in the south-east of Britain. They had also overestimated the total number of divisions in Britain by an astonishing fifty per cent.

Other parts of the Bodyguard operation included:

Zeppelin deception: invasion of the Balkans region using a mixture of fictitious armies, Polish and Soviet forces

Vendetta: plan for a landing in the South of France, launched from North Africa.

Ironside: landings near Bordeaux on the French west coast

Copperhead: The use of the actor M.E. Clifton James as Montgomery's double in Gibraltar and North Africa just prior to D-Day.

There were many sub-plans and actions within each strand and the overall operation was carried out using double agents, false communications, actual military build-ups and simulated ones, visual deception such as inflatable tanks and mock landing craft that would look real from aerial photography.

Prior to the invasion itself, the reconnaissance missions were on a large scale and audacious. Aerial photographs were taken by Spitfire planes sweeping low over the beaches, at great danger, in order to capture accurate imagery of the build-up of Rommel's beach defences. Sometimes, on the designated landing beaches, divers made stealth raids ashore under the cover of darkness in order to investigate the obstacles and take samples of sand. The latter was done to test if the beach would be able to hold the tanks that would be put ashore. Quite remarkably, following a BBC radio appeal in 1942, over ten million pre-war holiday beach photographs were sent in by the British public in order that they could be analysed by the invasion planners. The *Centurie* French Resistance network, which operated out of the Caen area, also relayed details of the beach defences back to London.

Bletchley Park, the secret complex north-west of London, which famously broke and decoded German communications using the 'Ultra' intercepts, reported on 2 June 1944 that the 'Latest evidence suggests enemy appreciates all Allied preparations completed. Expects initial landing Normandy or Brittany, followed by main effort in Pas de Calais.'

Bodyguard had worked.

'Let's Go'

The planned date for D-Day moved to 5 June. However, conditions on the 4th were poor: strong winds, heavy clouds and rough seas. These were nervous times; 156,000 men and thousands of tonnes of supplies and equipment were ready to ship across the Channel. How long could they be kept in a state of readiness? The longer they waited, the more chance of German discovery of the prepared fleet. The weather forecast for the next two weeks was less than favourable. Eisenhower, surely feeling an incredible burden, wrestled with the idea of postponing Overlord.

On the evening of 4 June, Group Captain James Stagg, a Royal Air Force meteorologist, met with Eisenhower. Stagg recommended a postponement of twenty-four hours; the weather on June 6, he predicted, would improve just enough for the Channel crossing to go ahead.

Improve *just enough* was right – it was far from perfect. On 5 June, 7,000 ships carrying their human invasion cargo headed to Area 'Z', the mid-Channel Assembly

54 *Visiting the Normandy Invasion Beaches and Battlefields*

area. Troops were anxious of course but many were suffering from debilitating sea-sickness due to the inclement weather.[6]

They waited.

Eisenhower hastily scribbled a message to be released in the event of failure. The words are a chilling reminder of the uncertainty of history:

> 'Our landings in the Cherbourg-Havre area have failed to gain a satisfactory foothold and I have withdrawn the troops. My decision to attack at this time and place was based upon the best information available. The troops, the air, and the navy did all that bravery and devotion to duty could do. If any blame or fault attaches to the attempt, it is mine alone.'

Group Captain James Stagg.

He mistakenly dated the note 5 July – as good an indicator as any as to the state of mental fatigue that he was suffering. That doom-laden message remained crumpled in Eisenhower's pocket.

At 2145 hours on 5 June, Eisenhower met with Stagg and received cautious but positive meteorological news. Then, addressing his staff, he uttered a simple phrase, but one on which the future of nations was dependent: 'OK, let's go.'

Eisenhower meets with men of the 101st Airborne shortly after giving the 'Let's go' for D-Day.

On 6 June, he sent a statement to all soldiers, sailors and airmen of the Expeditionary Force. He urged nothing less than full victory, the 'destruction of the German war machine' and the 'elimination of Nazi tyranny'.

As a reminder, if one were needed, he included the following gut-thudding, blood-pumping phrase:

'The eyes of the world are upon you.'

* * *

Footnotes:

1. As an interesting military history footnote, the American Civil War came briefly to Normandy when the Confederate commerce raider, CSS *Alabama*, was sunk in a battle with the USS *Kearsage* as it left Cherbourg harbour in 1864.
2. Do make time to sample this side of Normandy. Turbot, oysters, glorious cheeses and creamy sauces, moreish pastries, smooth cider and strong calvados – there are plenty of epicurean reasons to spend time in the region!
3. Literally, units full of men with hearing difficulties and stomach injuries.
4. By 1944 the *Wehrmacht* contained troops from Italy, France, Croatia, Poland, Finland, Hungary, Romania, Estonia, Latvia, Lithuania, North Africa, Russia, Ukraine, Crimea, Volga-Finns, Volga-Tatars and Indians. On D-Day itself, Lieutenant Robert Brewer of the 101st Airborne captured four Koreans fighting for the *Wehrmacht*. This baffling outcome must have been because they would have been in the Japanese Army in 1938, captured by the Soviets in 1939 and drafted into the Red Army before being captured during Barbarossa and subsequently forced into German uniform. It is entirely possible that they returned to Korea and then fought (possibly on different sides!?) during the Korean War. See Ambrose, *D-Day* p. 34
5. A secret wartime department tasked with military deception activities during the war.
6. One bonus of the poor weather was the German belief that an invasion was extremely unlikely at this time. *Luftwaffe* meteorological readings predicted two weeks of poor conditions. Extensive leave was granted along the French coastline, a number of *Wehrmacht* commanders attended a war gaming exercise in Rennes and Rommel headed to Germany to attend his wife's birthday!

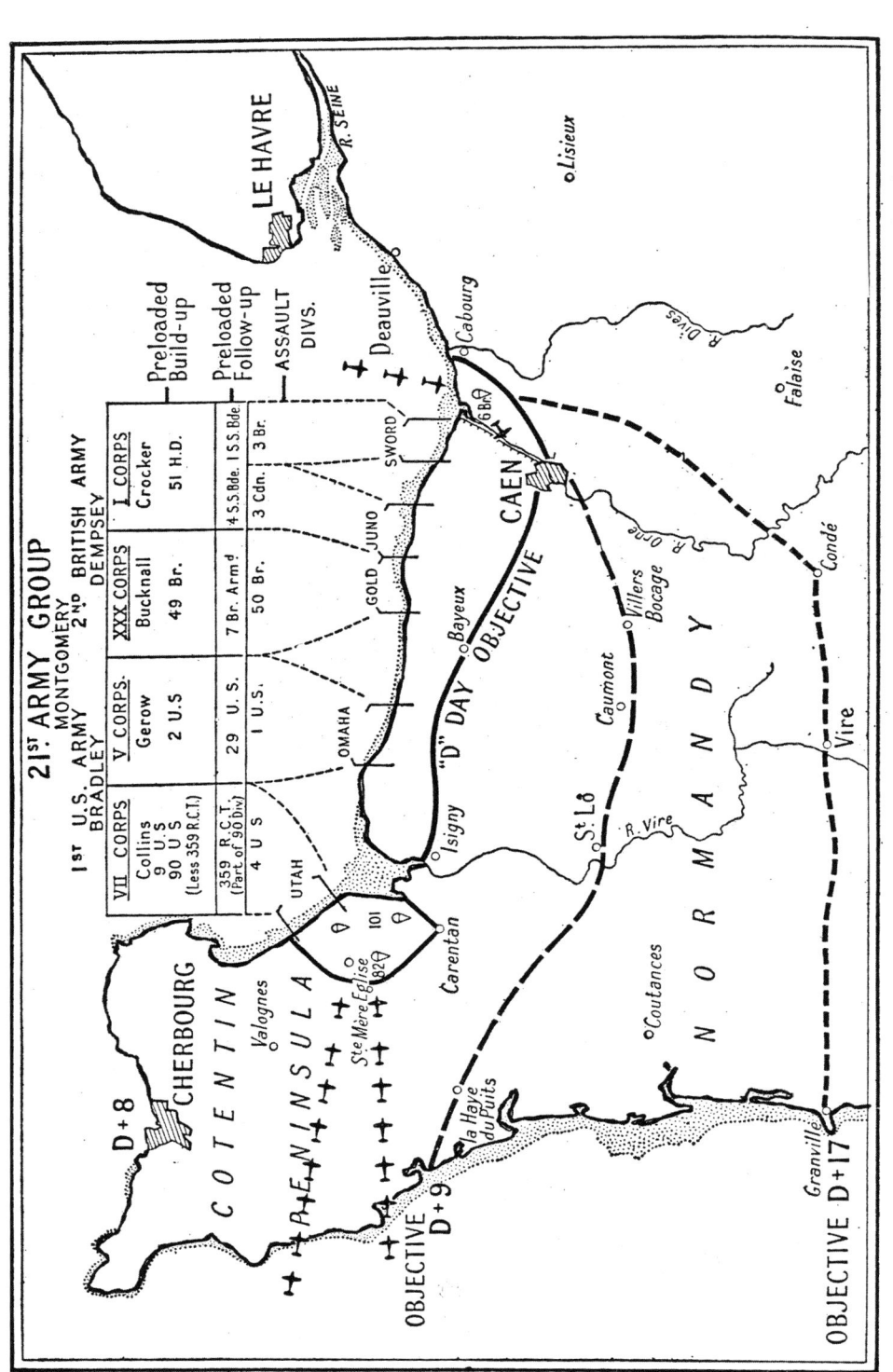

OPERATION NEPTUNE: THE ASSAULT PLAN

Tour One:
Utah and Omaha

One-Day Itinerary

Approximate start time of 0900 and end time of 1600.

To get to all of these sites in one day is possible, but requires good pace. All those sites given a letter addition (i.e. 1a, 1b) are, although highly recommended visits, those stops I would suggest better to leave out if time becomes an issue.

If you would rather take a more leisurely pace and prepare a lighter schedule, then you might only plan to visit the main stops (i.e. 1,2,3…) and if you find that you could do with adding another stop or two along the way then bring in the lettered stop closest to your current location (i.e. if you have just visited 3 then go to 3a). Furthermore, you can look for a museum to add in (see Museums chapter) and, for additional visits in order to extend the tour over more days, also see the 'Going further; doing more' chapter.

1. **Sainte-Mère-Église – town, church, pump**
   - 1a. US Airborne Museum
   - 1b. Statue of Lieutenant Richard 'Dick' Winters

2. **Utah Beach – beach, museum, memorials**

– LUNCH –

3. **La Cambe German Cemetery**
   - 3a. The Statue of Peace, Grandcamp Maisy

4. **Pointe du Hoc – site, bunkers, Rangers' Memorial**

5. **Dog Green Sector, Omaha Beach**

6. **The Normandy American Cemetery and Memorial**

– DAY END –

American Airborne Operations on D-Day

At 0130 hours, troops from the 82nd 'All American' and 101st 'Screaming Eagles' Divisions would be dropped north of the town of Carentan on the Cotentin Peninsula with the aim of securing the exits from Utah Beach and the crossings over the rivers Merderet and Douve.

The two divisions were made up of six infantry regiments which brought overall troop numbers to approximately 14,000 – over 800 planes were needed to transport them over their drop zones.

Major General Matthew B. Ridgway's 82nd Division had the specific tasks of taking the town of Sainte-Mère-Église, along with various bridges in the surrounding area, in order to establish a defensive line to repulse counter attacks. The 82nd were landing in an area of flooded marshlands, a precaution that the defending Germans had taken as a measure against such an invasion attempt.

Major General Maxwell D. Taylor's 101st were ordered to secure the beach exits for the seaborne forces and the landing zone for the division's gliders. After this, the next stage was to assault the town of Carentan.

Major General Matthew B. Ridgway.

Things did not go quite to plan for various reasons. Approximately thirty minutes before the main airborne landings, pathfinder teams parachuted in to locate the drop zones and set up radio and visual guides in order to help with the accuracy of the main jump. However, the cloud was dense and the weather generally poor and some of these teams landed in the wrong place, thus further hampering the accuracy of what would follow.

Major General Maxwell D. Taylor with 'Monty'.

When the main drops began the visibility remained an issue whilst, in addition to this, German anti-aircraft flak fire was of a sufficient enough intensity to force many inexperienced pilots of the C-47 Skytrains to take evasive action: many flew too fast, some too high and others too low. Many men of the 82nd came down in the flooded marshlands; weighed down by their equipment, some of these paratroopers never made it out of the bogs. Some landed right on top of the German 91st Division but, in general, they had a better drop than the 101st who were scattered over a very wide area which meant that they were only 20 per cent of their overall number when they first mustered on the ground.

However, Sainte-Mère-Église was captured by just after 0400 and the important bridge crossings secured; by 0600 the UTAH Beach exits were secured too. This was crucial: given the difficult terrain, a failure to secure these causeways over the marshland could have spelt disaster for the UTAH landings.

Despite the difficulties, the 'All American' and 'Screaming Eagles' had done a remarkable job.

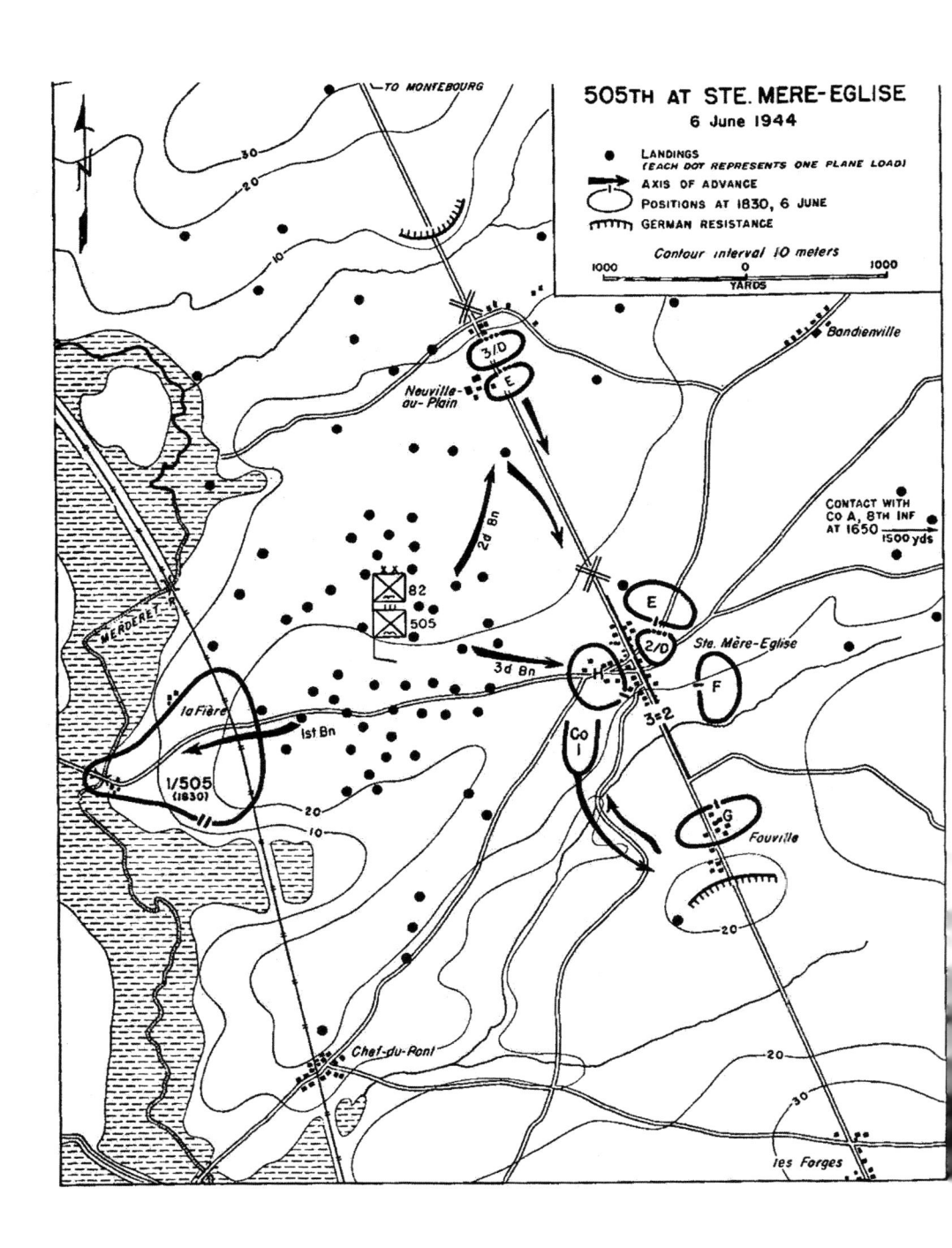

60 *Visiting the Normandy Invasion Beaches and Battlefields*

Utah and Omaha   61

1. Sainte-Mère-Église – town, church, pump

1 hour[1]

Lat & Long: 49.40399 – 1.31397

Sainte-Mère-Église is a small town that can be reached via the N13, north-west of Carentan. There is parking available in the central square near to the town church. As the Airborne Museum is opposite the church, this is where I would recommend that you park and start your day.

Context

An opportunity to set the scene for the rest of the day but to also consider the role of U.S. airborne operations in some detail. Given that the airborne operations were, chronologically, the first parts of the operation to unfold, it makes perfect sense to start the day here.

Orientation

Stand in any location in the town square with a good view of the church itself.

The church in Sainte-Mère-Église.

The Narrative

If this is the first stop on the first day of your tour:[2]

- Give a short version of the overview history of the war (pages 13–31) and a history of D-Day (pages 43–55)

Then, for all tours:

- Overview U.S. airborne operations (page 59).

Then:
This is Sainte-Mère-Église, a small town, founded in the eleventh century, which is located on a flat plain in the Cotentin Peninsula in Normandy.

On D-Day this was a crucial location as it straddled the N13 (Route Nationale 13) road, which was the only major road available for the German Army in moving reinforcements to assault Allied troop landings at Utah and Omaha Beaches. Part of *Mission Boston* (the American Airborne landings) was to capture and hold this town. Due to the bad weather and difficult approaches, many of the units involved missed their landing zones. However, the men of the 505th Parachute Infantry Regiment enjoyed an accurate jump – landing close to Sainte-Mère-Église.

Before getting to the capture of the town, let us consider the airborne operations a little more – especially from the point of view of the men who carried them out.

...

In the hours before departure, nerves were fraught. The twenty-four-hour delay had pushed some men, stationed near the airfields in their tented cities, to the edge. Scuffles occurred, tempers were close to the surface and many men simply wanted to get on with it rather than be shown another Hollywood movie reel in order to pass the time.

As the hour of departure drew nearer, an array of rituals began as men found ways to distract their minds from thinking too greatly about the overwhelming task ahead. Some daubed war paint across their faces and clipped their hair to emulate First Nation Apaches.

Men exchanged handshakes and letters for their loved ones, should they not return.

General Ridgway prayed.

Colonel Howard 'Skeets' Johnson whipped his men up into a frenzy, brandishing his knife, holding it aloft and promising that 'I swear to you that before tomorrow night this knife will be buried in the back of the blackest German in Normandy.'

As darkness engulfed the late evening of D-1, trucks carried paratroopers to the runways, stopping alongside each aircraft so that a stick (planeload)

of eighteen men could unload and, struggling under the considerable burden of their equipment, emplane. The paratroopers had to carry with them a miniature armaments and supply cache – alongside their helmet, main parachute and reserve parachute, it was common that men would be carrying the vast majority of the following: rifle; .45 automatic pistol; several knives; hundreds of rounds of ammunition; TNT; a small Hawkins mine for anti-tank work; entrenching tool; first-aid kits; morphine; gas mask; water; rations; grenades; blanket; raincoat; cigarettes; socks… and underwear.

These accoutrements of war almost doubled the weight of some individuals but very few men tried to surreptitiously discard their pack. The problem for the aggressor, carrying out an airborne assault by parachute is simple: although they have the element of surprise, after that they are on their own and simply cannot call on reinforcements until the next phase of the assault is a success. These men had to rely on their own ability to fight, capture critical objective points and hold them until others could relieve them. The reality was that the equipment they carried into battle was scarcely enough. Gliders would follow up with heavy weapon 'parapack' drops; but the airborne operation was vulnerable – nobody doubted that.

Shortly after 2200 hours, airfields across England began to rumble and then roar with a tumultuous cacophony of engines.

General Eisenhower had spent the evening with the Screaming Eagles at Welford airfield mingling with and encouraging those who would shortly be beginning their date with history. He watched and then saluted each aircraft that passed him by, as it took its place in the departure line. Then at 2245 the lead plane departed, followed in seven second intervals by forty-four more. They formed up into V patterns of nine planes and flew off into the inky darkness like some giant, quite beautiful, flock of birds.

A similar pattern repeated itself at over a dozen other airfields – 822 planes and 13,000 paratroopers were on their way.

As men – some in silence, others praying, some simply making those pointless but priceless little jokes that break the tension – endured that journey, they all had to find some kind of inner 'readiness', a quiet word with themselves, or their God, before the reckoning came.

Others vomited – part nerves, part the vibration and turbulence encountered.

General Maxwell Taylor, following the parachute tradition of senior commanders jumping with their men, lay down on the floor with some pillows.

Between 0115 to 0200 hours the aircraft all began to make their descents to 700 feet, ready for the drop.

General Ridgway, on board his C-47, looked around at the faces of the men and noted that they 'sat quietly, deep in their own thoughts […] nervousness and tension, and the cold that blasted through the open door, had its effect upon us all'.

As the planes descended and crossed over land, men began to focus on the features below – hedgerow upon hedgerow, streams and fields, quiet country lanes and inquisitive farm animals.

And then: chaos.

A vast bank of cloud had gathered over the Cotentin Peninsula, dead in the path of the flight routes for both the 82nd and 101st. For a few moments it caused havoc for this huge aerial convoy. Pilots lost sight of one another, many banked and plunged, fearing a collision. Going against orders, many pilots went to full throttle. Some men, already stood in position ready for the jump, were thrown like rag dolls around the cabin.

Almost as quickly as this disorientating bank of cloud had engulfed the aircraft it was passed through. However, many planes emerged into clarity only to find themselves off course, flying too low or too high or under direct fire from anti-aircraft guns below. And now it was time to jump.

If a jump went well, an aircraft could be emptied of its stick within ten seconds. Men would 'hook up', snapping their anchor line fastener into place, check their equipment, number off and then wait for the jumpmaster, crouched in the doorway, to give the order and flick the green light.

Not all jumps went so smoothly; as planes took evasive action and men, burdened under heavy packs, struggled to stay on their feet, some had to be literally bundled out by their colleagues. Some men, injured from direct fire, or the splinters of metal sheering off inside the cabins as a result of it, were unhooked and put to one side, hopefully to return back to Britain in time for treatment. At least one C-47 was blown into pieces, its occupants never getting the chance to make that jump at all. Many others were shot down after their stick had disembarked.

Only seven men were 'refusals' – they would face harsh repercussions and social ignominy.

Some 13,000 others were now floating down over Normandy.

The descent took approximately forty seconds. The unlucky ones suffered injuries on the way down – as gun fire crisscrossed the air, it was inevitable that some would take hits.

Some drowned, either in the flooded marshland or, as happened to at least one stick, because they were released into the sea at Utah beach.

One soldier, already on the ground, witnessed the results of a stick being released too low and thus with little time to deploy their parachutes: 'Seventeen men hit the ground before their chutes had time to open. They made a sound like large pumpkins being thrown down to burst against the ground.'

Others were luckier but suffered with impact injuries ranging from broken pelvises to cracked ribs and sprained ankles.

But, as these thousands of American feet began to touch the ground, the invasion-proper was underway.

Yet these first few hours were hugely confusing. Many soldiers, initially concerned with removing their cumbersome parachutes, felt a crushing wave of loneliness and fear as they tried to make sense of the darkness around them. Given the problems of the drop – the failure to establish accurate homing beacons, the cloud cover and the nerves of the pilots – the initial gathering together of formations was virtually impossible. Many men simply wandered about, using their 'clickers' or 'crickets' – the little metal toy given out to the men as a means of communicating in the darkness with one another – without success. Given the mix of adrenaline, lack of sleep and drugs (Drapomine air-sickness pills), many were dead tired – some did literally find a hedgerow or a quiet spot in a field and slept for an hour or two.

Some went off 'Kraut-hunting', stalking German machine gun positions and destroying them with grenades.

Approximately 3,000 soldiers in each division were lost or dead. These hours of darkness were filled with disorientation but, crucially, on the whole the Germans did little to reveal their positions and thus the Americans had time, through luck, endeavour and leadership, to scrabble groups together in readiness for assaults on their targets.

...

Sainte Mère-Église

The scenes that played out here have been made famous through the iconic imagery of the 1962 film *The Longest Day*.

Just before 0100 on 6 June, a house was ablaze in this stone-built town, caused by the Allied air raids prior to the airborne assault. The swastika flag, hanging from the town hall, was also on fire.

Under the watchful eye of German soldiers, the local population had been raised from their beds and, drawing water from the pump in the central square (the Place de l'Église), were in the midst of attempting to subdue the flames when attention turned to the lit-up sky above them.

At approximately 0145 some men from the 82nd had been mistakenly dropped above the town, their misfortune compounded by the flames acting as a torchlight for the Germans below.[3]

Two men fell directly into the flames of the burning house.[4] Several more hung on roofs and from trees. German soldiers shot many as they floated down or hung helplessly. Famously, Private John 'Buck' Steele, a thirty-one-year-old barber from Illinois, caught on the church spire. He had also been shot through the foot on his descent. Germans took pot shots at him whilst he feigned death, whilst the constant ringing of the church bell meant that he would be deaf for many days afterwards. He was eventually cut down by the soldiers operating the German machine gun position in the spire of the church and held until he was liberated later in the day.

Yet what happened next was quite astonishing. The German garrison, after capturing a dozen or so Allied soldiers, went back to bed! They had failed to grasp that this was the invasion. Whilst they went back to their rest, close to 1,000 Allied soldiers were gathering in fields nearby, preparing to take the town.

At 0255 the German anti-aircraft battery left the town.

All was quiet for an hour or so until, at approximately 0400, Mayor Alexandre Renaud,

The effigy of Private John Steele.

watching from his bedroom window, spotted the movement of soldiers – but from whose side were they?

These were likely soldiers of the 3rd Battalion, 505th Regiment (3rd/505th) led by Lieutenant Colonel Edward Krause. He had set up roadblocks on the outskirts of the village and led a small detachment into the town itself. After severing the main German communication cable to Cherbourg, he carried out house to house searches and captured thirty Germans who had gone back to bed. Many more simply ran from the town.

At 0415 Alexandre Renaud received a knock on the door. A paratrooper captain offered him chewing gum.

Sainte Mère-Église was the first French town to be liberated.

John Steele – 20th anniversary of D-Day.

Activities

Stained glass window memorial.   *The town pump!*

Explore the town. An effigy of John Steele hangs from the Church and there are two glorious stained glass windows, that are best viewed from inside the church, which memorialise the events of that night. One of them depicts the Virgin Mary surrounded by paratroopers and the other carries the inscription *Ils sont revenus* ('They have come back'). John Steele returned to the town periodically after the war and became quite famous due to his iconic experience and subsequent prominence in *The Longest Day*. The pump from which townspeople drew the water to tackle the flames still stands in Place de l'Église. There is an array of information boards and memorials in the town, with many good cafés and souvenir shops around the central square.

In front of the old town hall you will notice a round, stone monument that is the first of a series of markers of the 'Voie de la Liberté' – indicating the advance of US forces across France which ends at Bastogne.

Also, if you locate the fire station you will be able to find a marker behind it for one of the original US cemeteries – the bodies were removed after the war, either to be repatriated or to be buried in one of the two large American Cemeteries in Normandy.

1a. US Airborne Museum

1 hour

The museum is located in Place de l'Église.

14 rue Eisenhower
50480 Sainte-Mère-Église
Tel. +33 2 33 41 41 35
Fax. +33 2 33 41 78 87
infos@airborne-museum.org
http://www.airborne-museum.org

Context

There are so many good museums in the D-Day landing areas and periphery that I have chosen not to recommend many of them within the itineraries. Instead you can look them up in the later chapter and decide which to add in to your travels as you see fit.

However, this is an excellent stop and will add much to your day. It takes the explanation of the various American Airborne assaults further and in far more detail and contains an array of memorabilia as well as useful audio-visual content/ experiences. The C47 Aircraft *Argonia* is on display in an impressive hanger that is shaped like a delta parachute. There is also a restored original Waco CG-4A Hadrian glider.

1b. Statue of Lieutenant Richard 'Dick' Winters

10 minutes

Lat & Long: 49.39143 – 1.21344

The monument can be found on the D913, 50480 Sainte-Marie-du-Mont and is approximately 15 minutes from Sainte-Mère-Église.

68 *Visiting the Normandy Invasion Beaches and Battlefields*

From the Airborne Museum at Sainte-Mère-Église, head south-west on Rue Eisenhower/D17 towards Rue Général de Gaulle/Voie de la Liberté/D974. Turn left onto Rue Général de Gaulle/Voie de la Liberté/D974.

After 800m, at the roundabout take the 2nd exit onto the D67. Follow this for 5km before turning right on to the D115 and then right on to the D14. After a few minutes you will come to the junction with the D913. Turn left on to the D913 and the statue is just a minute or so further up on your left.

Context

A stunning statue to memorialize leadership and the commanding officer of Easy Company, who was made famous by Stephen E. Ambrose's book and the subsequent HBO mini-series, *Band of Brothers*. It was unveiled in 2012.

'Dick' Winters leadership memorial.

Orientation

The statue is close to Ste Marie du Mont, which was an objective for Easy Company.

Narrative

Richard 'Dick' Winters enlisted in the US Army following his graduation in 1941. He had volunteered in the hope that it would mean a shorter term of military service and that he would avoid any later draft.

The man himself – Richard 'Dick' Winters.

During his officer training Winters decided to join the parachute infantry and was assigned to Company E, 2nd Battalion, 506th Parachute Infantry Regiment, 101st Airborne Division at Camp Toccoa, Georgia. The training at Toccoa, led by First Lieutenant Herbert Sobel, was brutal, with high rates of drop-out amongst the men.

In late 1943 Easy Company transferred to Aldbourne in England in order to prepare for D-Day.

It was here that concerns over Sobel's leadership abilities came to a head and led to his transfer out of Easy and replacement by First Lieutenant Thomas Meehan.

At approximately 0115 hours on 6 June 1944, the C-47 carrying Meehan was shot down over Normandy, exploding upon impact with a hedgerow, killing all on board.

Winters, who had prayed almost the entire flight in his C-47, carried out a successful jump, landing close to Sainte Mére-Église. Because of Meehan's death he became the de facto commanding officer of Easy Company.

Winters carried out a number of brave actions on D-Day, none more so than during an attack that became known as the Brécourt Manor Assault.

Brécourt Manor was a large farm with a German gun battery located in hedgerows nearby and just north of Ste Marie du Mont. There was conflicting information as to what type of guns were there and how well defended it was. However, the guns were firing on to the exit routes from Utah Beach and so it was imperative that the position was neutralized.

Winters led a team of thirteen men against the fifty in the battery. The Germans were well ensconced within a trench system, with mortars and a clear field of fire for their machine guns. Winters' men had a light mortar, two light machine guns, a couple of Tommy guns and several rifles.

Using the two light machine guns and mortar fire to pin down the Germans, Winters led a lightning quick flanking manoeuvre as the squad entered the hedgerow trench system and went from gun pit to gun pit, silencing what turned out to be 105mm howitzers with explosives.

Winters then withdrew his men as German machine guns increased their fire upon them; but not before securing a map detailing German gun positions around Utah. Then, two US Sherman tanks appeared, en route from Utah Beach. Winters leapt on to one and demanded that they destroy everything in the hedgerows and beyond.

This they did.

The Brécourt Manor gun battery was no more.

On 1 July Richard Winters was promoted to Captain and the next day General Omar N. Bradley awarded him the Distinguished Service Cross – the second highest military honour that can be awarded to a member of the US Army.

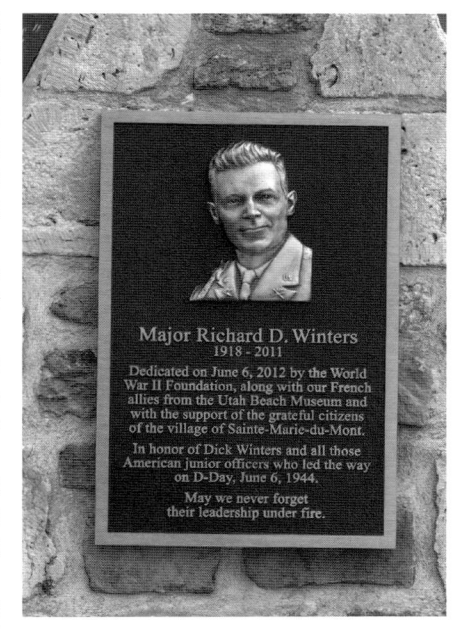

Winters would go on to take part in Operation Market Garden, the defence of Bastogne during the Battle of the Bulge and the capture of Berchtesgarden.

Just before midnight on 6 June, Winters lay down to rest at Ste Marie du Mont and, just like he had done twenty-four hours before, he prayed to God, thanking him for his protection during the day and asking for his help in the next one. He also promised to himself that if he survived the war he would spend the rest of his life living a quiet existence on a little farm somewhere.

This he did until his retirement in 1997.

It was during that decade that Winters became a well-known and engaging figure, whose experiences of the war inspired many. Historian Stephen E. Ambrose brought Winters' actions, and that of Easy Company, to vivid life in the book *Band of Brothers*. The HBO series, in which actor Damian Lewis plays Winters, is still one of the most memorable and moving visual depictions of the war.

His actions at the Brécourt Manor Assault are still studied at the West Point US Military Academy as a textbook example of small-unit flanking operations against a force of superior numbers.

Winters was a very humble man, downplaying his actions as simply doing what was necessary and expected of him.

He died in 2011 and thus sadly never got to see this statue unveiled. It is twelve feet tall and made from bronze. Winters only agreed to a statue being made of him if it was dedicated to all the junior officers who served during the Normandy campaigns.

This is a statue to commemorate and recognize leadership.

In the closing scenes of the *Band of Brothers* series, the real soldiers who had been depicted in the episodes, at that point in their seventies and eighties, make some closing remarks to camera. Winters quoted from a letter that Mike Ranney, a friend and fellow member of Easy Company during the war, wrote to him in 1982:

> 'I cherish the memories of a question my grandson asked me the other day when he said, 'Grandpa, were you a hero in the war?' Grandpa said 'No…but I served in a company of heroes.'

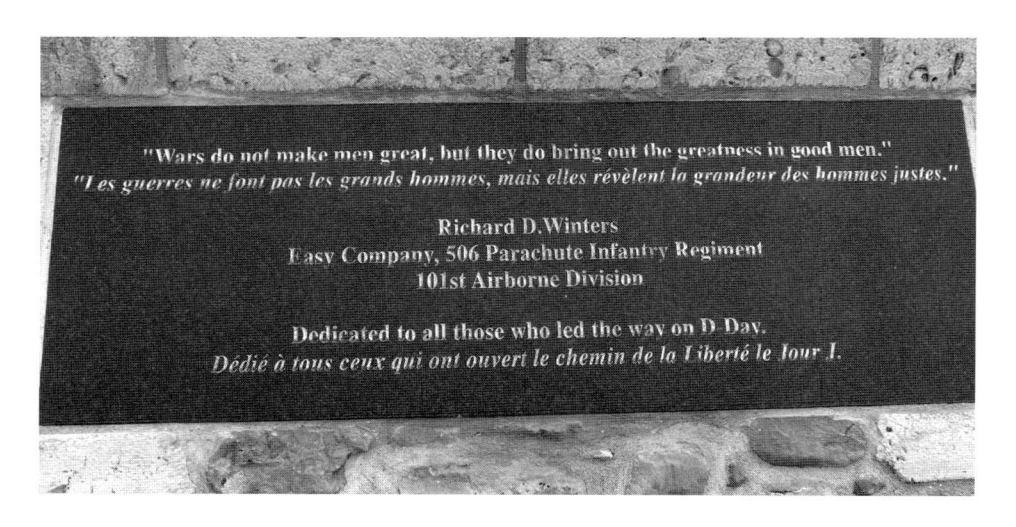

"Wars do not make men great, but they do bring out the greatness in good men."
"Les guerres ne font pas les grands hommes, mais elles révèlent la grandeur des hommes justes."

Richard D. Winters
Easy Company, 506 Parachute Infantry Regiment
101st Airborne Division

Dedicated to all those who led the way on D-Day.
Dédié à tous ceux qui ont ouvert le chemin de la Liberté le Jour J.

Activities

Prior to your visit it would be useful to have read *Band of Brothers* or to watch the series, in particular the first few episodes, which cover the training, build up and first drop of the invasion. I have found this to be an excellent DVD box-set to show on the coach for trips involving long stretches of travel.

American Operations at Utah Beach

Utah Beach was the westerly most beach of those to be assaulted on D-Day. It is on the Cotentin Peninsula, west of the rivers Douve and Vire. The importance of this sector lay in sealing off the Peninsula, preventing the Germans from reinforcing Cherbourg.

Major General J. Lawton Collins' VII Corps attack would be made by troops of the 4th Infantry Division – approximately 21,000 men. They would be opposed by two battalions of the 919th Grenadier Regiment, largely made up of deeply unreliable *Osttruppen* troops. Held further back inland was the US 91st Infantry Division.

The plan was for an initial heavy bombing raid on German entrenchments and gun emplacements that constituted the Atlantic Wall defences, followed by the troop landings supported with shell-fire from naval vessels. The designated assault zones were named Tare Green and Uncle Red; both were approximately 1,000 yards wide and led to beach exits that had to be secured in order that the troops could get off the beach itself.

At 0200 the leading edge of the invasion forces began to appear off the coast of Normandy – the minesweepers. At 0230, eleven miles off the Utah Beach coast line, the order was given to troop carrying ships to load the LCVP landing crafts (or Higgins Boats); this embarking of human cargo took place between 0300–0400 hours. This in itself was not an easy task at all – the sea was choppy and accidents did happen; be it men falling and breaking limbs or, far worse, slipping into the sea and being dragged under by the weight of the kit they carried.

Due to problems with visibility and a quite natural fear of some in Bomber Command of 'friendly fire' incidents (dropping bombs on the landing craft below), some of the aerial bombardment missed its target – but those bombers flying at a lower altitude were remarkably accurate.

The LCVPs began to make the torturous three-hour journey to shore, enduring four feet high waves which caused vomiting amongst many of the poor souls on board. Thirty-six men could be crammed into each boat and most longed to get off them as soon as they could.

At about 0530 hours German gun batteries opened up and by 0550 the full Allied Naval bombardment was under way.

H-Hour was 0630 and the lead troops kept to this schedule perfectly, supported by high explosive drenching fire from shallow water vessels in support; the idea was to keep the German defensive positions pinned down whilst the troops made their first moves from the boat to land.

Troops from the 8th Infantry Regiment were the first to get Normandy sand on their boots. They looked ahead at a hundred yards of beach – relatively open beach. They began to beat a path across the sand under some, but not unduly heavy, fire.

Within minutes, fifty-two LCVPs had come ashore and at H-Hour+15 minutes, twenty-eight dual-drive (DD) tanks were landed.

Brigadier General Theodore Roosevelt Jr – eldest son of former President Theodore Roosevelt (1901–1909), arthritic, suffering a heart condition and, at fifty-six, the oldest man to take part in D-Day – landed with a first wave assault company and immediately realized a problem: they were on the wrong beach!

Due to the poor weather, strong current and shell-fire affecting visibility, they had come ashore at the Victor sector of Utah Beach – approximately 2,000 yards south of where they should have been.

Roosevelt had to make a quick decision: somehow move the attack to the correct location or stay where they were. He decided to stick, his famous order being the simple yet powerful: 'We're going to start the war from right here.' Roosevelt cut an inspirational, if somewhat eccentric, figure as he spent the next couple of hours striding up and down the beach, cane in hand, exhorting his men forward. He relayed poetry, tales about his father – anything to calm the men and get them moving forward. He would be given the Medal of Honor for his actions.[5]

Ultimately, the incorrect beach landing was of huge benefit to the landing forces. This area was far less fortified and defended than the intended location.

Theodore Roosevelt Jr.

By 0930, three of the four beach exits had been secured and by midday troops had been able to link up with men from the 101st Airborne near the village of Poupeville, a couple of miles from the beachhead itself. To the west, the link with the 82nd Airborne at Sainte-Mère-Église was not possible until D+1.

The landings at Utah were an unquestionable success. A six-mile penetration from the beach itself was secured and 21,000 troops landed at the cost of only 197 casualties.

2. Utah Beach – beach, museum, memorials

2 hours

From the statue of Lieutenant Richard 'Dick' Winters simply continue along the D913 for 4km and you will arrive at the Utah Beach Museum and Memorial complex.

Utah Beach Museum
Utah Beach
50480 Sainte-Marie-du-Mont
Tel: +33 2 33 71 53 35
Fax: +33 2 33 71 92 36
www.utah-beach.com
Lat & Long: 49.40318 -1.19619

Utah and Omaha 73

Utah Beach museum and memorials.

Context

A superb museum, numerous memorials and an opportunity to visit the beach itself.

Orientation

It is a good idea to head down to the beach itself in order to set the scene for the museum visit. The route to the beach is signposted – but it is obvious in any case.

The Narrative

First:

- Give a version of American Operations on Utah Beach (pages 71–2)

Then:

This is Utah Beach. One of the first things you will notice is the lack of any steep cliffs at the end of the beach; most unlike the topography at Omaha which you will see later.

The museum itself is built on top of three German bunkers that formed part of the Resistance Nest structure, known as WN5.

Erwin Rommel had visited this site in May 1944 in order to inspect the quality of the Atlantic Wall obstacles and emplacements. He was far from happy at what he perceived to be a far too lightly fortified position. Twenty-three-year-old Lieutenant Arthur Jahnke, the man in command of WN5 and the seventy-five soldiers placed there, was instructed by Rommel to remove his gloves.

When Rommel saw the many cuts and bruises that decorated Jahnke's palms, Rommel's anger subsided and he thanked him for his efforts in preparing to defend the Reich.

On the morning of June 6, Jahnke was awoken from his slumber by the sounds of airplanes and nearby gun fire. A patrol returned with a group of captured American Airborne troops but they gave nothing away to Jahnke.

Then at 0550 Jahnke's world was turned upside down by the hell-fire and brimstone of the mass aerial and naval bombardment. By 0615, WN5's large guns were neutralised: direct hits had destroyed them, emplacements were damaged and many men were killed or incapacitated.

A wounded Jahnke looked out to sea and must have felt his stomach drop at the sight before him: the invasion was underway.

As Jahnke tried to muster a defence by shifting rubble and digging trenches, American troops landed. One minute after the first troops landed, Brigadier General Roosevelt was on the beach, encouraging his men forward.

Engineers blew a hole in the sea wall and American troops stormed WN5. Within one hour of landing, the beach was secure and the German positions overlooking the beach cleared.

Jahnke and a small detachment of men held out until midday in the dunes beyond the beach. He was captured by American soldiers and survived the war. He returned to WN5 in 1987 and met with an American soldier who had stormed the beach with the first troops all those years before.

Then leave the beach and have a look at the many interesting and impressive monuments and memorials. You will see:

- The Federal Monument of the United States of America
- US Navy Normandy Monument
- Monument of the 4th Infantry Division
- Monument of the 90th Infantry Division
- Memorial to the 1st Engineer Special Service Brigade
- A memorial crypt underneath the bunker
- Milestone 00 – marks the start of the Liberty Road to Bastogne
- Memorial Higgins – an excellent addition to the site. A gift by the people of Columbus, Nebraska, the birthplace of Andrew Higgins, designer of the LCVP Higgins landing craft.

There are a number of commemorative plaques, a light anti-aircraft gun and a Sherman tank. The café and bar *Le Roosevelt* is well worth a visit; it serves refreshments and good simple food but it is also full of nostalgic displays, photos and exhibits.

Then visit the outstanding museum – certainly one of the author's favourites in Normandy. The museum structure itself is impressive, as are the multiple exhibits that chart the invasion in its entirety, whilst detailing the Utah landings in impressive detail.

The museum was opened in 1962 due to the vision and dedication of Michel de Vallavieille, Mayor of Saint Marie du Mont. It was extended in 1964 and a theatre added in 1984. An extraordinary occurrence took place in 2007 when David and Gene Dewhurst visited the museum on a family trip.[6] Dumbfounded, they recognized a photograph of their father, Major David Dewhurst, posing in front of a B-36 Marauder. Major Dewhurst had led one of the final aerial bombing flights over WN5 just before ground troops made it to the beach. After the war Major Dewhurst was killed by a drunk driver and thus the two sons never really got to know their father.

Completely inspired by their visit, the brothers contributed millions of dollars to help the museum to finance a massive expansion project. This was realized in 2011 when the museum reopened. A beautiful hanger containing a B-26 Marauder was at the heart of the redevelopment, alongside new oral histories, an original Higgins boat and a documentary called 'Victory in the Sand'.

I would also note that the staff at Utah Beach museum are first rate – knowledgeable and very friendly. You will not be disappointed with your visit here.

Utah Beach.

3. La Cambe German Cemetery

30 minutes

14230 La Cambe, France
Lat & Long: 49.34304 -1.02598

Leave Utah Beach museum on the D913 and keep on this for 5.5km. Head into Sainte-Marie-du-Mont but continue through on the D913 and keep on this for a further 6km. Take the slip road for Caen/Isigny-sur-Mer and join the N13. Stay on this for 21km and then take the D113 exit to La Cambe/Vouilly. Take the first exit at the roundabout. After 110 metres turn left. You will see the cemetery parking.

Context

One of the largest German cemeteries in Normandy.

Narrative

Initially there were two adjacent burial grounds on this site. One contained burials of American servicemen and the other German. However, after the war ended, two-thirds of the American burials were repatriated and those remaining were moved to the Normandy American Cemetery at Colleville-sur-Mer.

The German War Graves Commission (*Volksbund Deutsche Kriegsgräberfürsorge*) decided to establish six major burial sites in Normandy. This one, La Cambe, would be one of the largest.

The mound over the **Kameradaengrab.**

Then read about the work of the Volksbund Deutsche Kriegsgräberfürsorge *(pages 37–8).*

In 1954 work began here that eventually saw 12,000 bodies exhumed from 1,400 locations and brought to be buried on this site. Work was finished in 1961. In 1996 the information centre and peace garden opened, along with the planting of twenty-one maple trees; there are now 1,200 such trees. As a symbol of reconcilitaion and renewal, the Royal British Legion sponsor the first maple tree to the left of the entrance into the cemetery.

There are 21,222 burials, with 296 men buried in a mass grave (*Kameradaengrab*) under the mound at the centre of the cemetery. On top of that mound is a cross and two figures – parents mourning for their loss.

Flat stones mark the graves of those below – usually four or more mentioned together, so as to save space.

Everywhere is dark, grey and solemn.

The result, as with German cemeteries of the Great War, is a sense of brooding, loss and sheer sadness.

However, how are we meant to feel about walking a cemetery such as this? This is a difficult question to answer and many struggle to make sense of their feelings here.

The sign upon entering the cemetery reads: 'The German Cemetery at La Cambe: In the Same Soil of France. Until 1947, this was an American cemetery. The remains were exhumed and shipped to the United States. It has been German since 1948, and contains over 21,000 graves. With its melancholy rigour, it is a graveyard for soldiers not all of whom had chosen either the cause or the fight. They too have found rest in our soil of France.'

La Cambe German Cemetery.

Yes, they are soldiers fighting a war and many of them did not choose their cause; however, surely many here were committed Nazis too? This is the problem with history and its fundamental importance too – we should not find it easy to come to a judgment here; this is a difficult place to be. Yet it is vital that we remember these men and what brought them here to die if we are to do justice to what this war was and to develop our understanding of the world.

Activities

Walk the cemetery and think about the points raised above.

One of the most notable burials is that of *SS-Hauptsturmführer* Michael Wittmann, who was a *Waffen-SS* tank commander and a recipient of the highest award given for battlefield bravery by the Nazis: the Knight's Cross of the Iron Cross with Oak Leaves and Swords. Adolf Hitler personally awarded this to him. He is most famous for destroying fourteen tanks and fifteen personnel carriers in fifteen minutes during the Battle of Villers-Bocage on 13 June 1944. He was killed in his tank on 8 August 1944 but there is much speculation amongst historians as to who got the fatal shot, given his notoriety and somewhat controversial fame.

Visit the good information centre and peace garden. This is a cemetery that school students, in particular, need a great deal of time to think about.

3a. The Statue of Peace, Grandcamp Maisy

10 minutes

30 Route de Vierville
14450 Grandcamp-Maisy
Lat & Long: 49.38799 -1.03141

Leaving La Cambe, head south towards Ferme de Romilly and continue on to Le Vieux Château for 1km. Then turn right on to the D199 and stay on this for 5.5km before turning tight on to the Rue de la Haulte Voie/D514. After a few minutes you will see the statue on your left.

Context

A rather striking statue and an opportunity to consider peace amidst the war. Also, a place of extraordinary personal bravery.

The Statue of Peace.

Narrative

This is a ten feet high, eight-ton statue made of oxidized steel that was sculptured by Chinese artist Yao Yan.

He created a Statue of Peace for Korea in 1995, for Russia in 2000 and, in 2001, a stainless-steel World Peace Statue, which stands on Friendship Square in Beijing.

This one was inspired by the Normandy landings; but was more specifically chosen to be sited here due to the US Army Ranger actions at Pointe du Hoc. It was dedicated in 2004 during the sixtieth anniversary of D-Day.

The colours are symbolic: the white steel and the sky blue are the colours of peace and reason in the face of injustice and war; the red granite of the pedestal symbolizes the blood shed during the war; the green of the lawn is an image of tranquillity and serenity.

The front of the World Peace Statue is marked with two Chinese characters, one meaning modesty and harmony, the other peace and tranquillity.

The structure also resembles the Chinese ideograms which signify harmony and balance, serenity, tranquillity and calm, and the western letters 'V' for victory, stretching out like two arms embracing the world and 'W' (for world, worship, warm). Eastern harmony is balanced by Western equality, fraternity and liberty.

The translated message is: 'When we all want peace, Why is the world full of conflict? Why are endless wars still ravaging the earth? Why do famine, poverty and plague still keep humanity in bondage? Citizens of this global community love our earth! Together let us stop war and live in harmony!'

Activities

A quick photo stop.

However, you may want to visit the Sergeant Peregory Memorial which is just in front of the statue. This marks the place where Frank Peregory won a Medal of Honor because of his actions on 8 June when, using grenades and a bayonet, he assaulted a German entrenched position, capturing thirty-five enemy soldiers and clearing the way for leading elements of 3rd Battalion, 116th Regiment to advance.

Official citation:

> 'On 8 June 1944, the 3rd Battalion of the 116th Infantry was advancing on the strongly held German defences at Grandcamp-Maisy, France, when the leading elements were suddenly halted by decimating machine gun fire from a firmly entrenched enemy force on the high ground overlooking the town. After numerous attempts to neutralize the enemy position by supporting artillery and tank fire had proved ineffective, T/Sgt.[7] Peregory, on his own initiative, advanced up the hill under withering fire, and worked his way to the crest where he discovered an entrenchment leading to the main enemy fortifications 200 yards away. Without hesitating, he leaped into the trench and moved toward the emplacement. Encountering a squad of enemy riflemen, he fearlessly attacked them with hand grenades and bayonet, killed 8 and forced 3 to surrender. Continuing along the trench, he single-handedly forced the surrender of 32 more riflemen, captured the machine gunners, and opened the way for the leading elements of the battalion to advance and secure its objective. The extraordinary gallantry and aggressiveness displayed by T/Sgt. Peregory are exemplary of the highest tradition of the armed forces.'

Peregory was killed in action six days later. He is buried in the Normandy American Cemtery and Memorial: Plot G, row 21, grave 7.

Map depicting the planned and actual first wave landings on Omaha Beach.

American Operations at Omaha Beach

On the original COSSAC plans (and until the addition of Utah) Omaha was the westernmost assault beach and at over 7,000 yards was the largest of the beaches to be attacked. It was also extremely well defended and fortified, including fifteen particular strongpoints. The beaches themselves were full of obstacles, ranging from Belgian gates to mines and Czech hedgehogs and, once these were traversed, the beach was backed by dauntingly high bluffs. This was far different to the German position at Utah. There were five exit slips from the beach and securing these would be vital to the success, or failure, on this beach.

The US V Corps was given the task of landing two regimental combat teams on to the beach. Omaha was divided into ten sections, codenamed (from west to east): Charlie, Dog Green, Dog White, Dog Red, Easy Green, Easy White, Easy Red, Fox Green, Fox White and Fox Red. The western half of the beach was the responsibility of the 116th Regimental Combat Team of the untested 29th Infantry Division and nine US Army Ranger companies.[8] The 29th Division was a National Guard division, similar to British Territorials, and was made up of men who joined together from the same geographical locations. The eastern section was the target of the heavily experienced 1st Infantry Division – the 'Big Red One'. Attached to these forces were artillery, tanks, the Special Engineer Brigade and Force B of the Ranger Assault Group. Force A of the Ranger Assault Group had the daunting objective of capturing a coastal battery at Pointe du Hoc – a promontory that, at a hundred feet, was the highest point between Utah and Omaha beaches. Over 40,000 soldiers were to be used in one way or another in the Omaha assault.

The Headquarters of American V Corps knew the difficulty facing them, as noted in their war diary: 'The attempt to do what had been contemplated by all the great military leaders of modern European History – a cross channel invasion – was about to commence.'

Facing the Americans was the German 352nd Division at a strength of approximately 12,000. However, only two of its key infantry battalions and a light artillery battalion were actually close to Omaha Beach. The rest were spread out over 250 square miles between the mouth of the River Vire and Arromanches.[9] There were a large number of teenage soldiers in this group but, crucially, fifty per cent of the division were experienced troops, including many veterans of the Eastern Front campaigns.

On D-Day, action began off the coast of Omaha just before 0100 hours, when minesweepers began their work. The heavy bombardment ships were in place at 0220 hours, with transport vessels arriving forty-five minutes later. The difficult unloading process into the LCVPs began and at 0430 they began their eleven-mile journey to shore. The landing craft that would hit the beaches first set off from a little closer to shore at 0520.

As they approached the beaches, the wind and tide began to drag the landing craft eastwards. At H-Hour-50 minutes, amphibious DD tanks were launched from their LCTs; but from 4.5km out at sea. These specially adapted Sherman tanks had a propeller and inflatable canvas screen and were an incredibly innovative part of the 'Hobart's Funnies' tank adaptions. The idea was to be able to provide tank support to the infantry immediately, rather than in a later follow-up landing.

Given the turbulent seas, this decision to launch from so far out turned out to be a disaster. The DDs intended for Dog Green, Dog White, Dog Red and Easy Green were swamped by the swell and promptly sank. Of thirty-two tanks, only five made it to shore. However, all thirty-two tanks for Easy Red and Fox Green did arrive safely, as their commanders did not have to risk the open seas but were, instead, delivered onto the beach.

Captain Scott-Bowden, on his craft heading to Omaha Beach, suddenly became aware of the 329 heavy bomber planes coming overhead to target German positions, particularly on the exit draws. Much to his chagrin, the bombing was wildly inaccurate, largely hitting the fields beyond the bluffs. 'That's a fat lot of use, all it will do is wake them up.' The over-optimism in precision aerial bombing was a feature of D-Day. It is also important to remember the casualties it caused to the French civilian population, 3,000 of whom died in the first twenty-four hours of the invasion – including the nine-month-old baby of the baker of Vierville, killed by a bomb from an Allied plane.

The landing craft came under direct and intense fire approximately 1,000 yards from the beaches. Given the sea conditions and the weight of the naval bombardment obscuring views, all but a handful of troops landed on the correct section of beach; one company even ended up on Gold Beach.

This was an ominous start.

Not only had the landing craft become confused and jumbled but, quite often, they grounded a distance from shore, which led to many men jumping into deep water and then being pulled under by the weight of their kit.

Pinging, thudding and screeching noises intensified as bullets began to pepper the craft. Men began to be hit even before the ramps were dropped.

And then those ramps did fall…

Direct and concentrated German machine gun fire began to cut down men before they had a chance to move. Some scrambled for cover, others jumped over the side and took a gamble with the depth of water. Some men got trapped under the ramps themselves. Bullets slashed through the water, killing and wounding many who were wading or swimming the final distance.

Very soon there were dozens of dead men floating all around. Those who were living tried to use these corpses for shelter, others pretended to be dead, hoping that the tide would then float them in.

For those lucky enough to make it ashore, the task was daunting.

German fire rained down upon the men from up on top of the cliffs and from the flanks either side of the beach. Added to this there were over 200 yards of beach to cross in order to attain some cover under the sea wall. Beyond the sea wall was a stretch of marshy grassland, with bluffs beyond that ranged from 100–150 feet in height. There were five exits or 'draws' that led off the beach.

Men scrambled for cover behind the defences. Some men, horribly wounded, just lay where they were. Others, clearly in a state of mental shock induced by the carnage and, more often than not, suffering a severe wound, walked haphazardly around the beach until they were either grabbed and shaken back into reality or cut down by the bullets.

Many veterans vividly remember the sound of the bullets hitting the wet sand: 'sip-sip'. They also remember the screams.

A common theme when one speaks to veterans, or reads about men at war, is the notion of time slowing down during intense combat. Many Omaha Beach survivors speak this way.[10]

The follow-up waves of the attack came across scenes of utter horror when their ramps dropped; officers had to summon up extraordinary bravery and confidence in order to get their men moving. Those in the first waves who were still alive and had made it to the sea wall, watched in helplessness and horror as these later waves of craft beached – it was like some demented blood-sport and they were the spectators.

Colonel Charles Canham and Brigadier General Norman D. Cota had landed at 0730 on Dog White. Their inspirational leadership was one of the highlights of American bravery on the day. Using Company C of the 116th Infantry and the 5th Ranger Battalion, who had meant to land on Dog Green but had drifted to Dog White, Cota and Canham led an assault against the bluffs from about 0800 hours. Canham was shot through the wrist whilst trying to

Colonel Charles D.W. Canham.

find an exit from the beach – he simply bandaged it and put his arm in a sling whilst continuing to exhort his men to 'Go kill some goddamned Krauts!'

They had to get off the beach.

As Colonel George A. Taylor said that day: 'Two kinds of people are staying on this beach, the dead and those about to die – now let's get the hell out of here.'

It was leadership that mattered in scenarios such as this: galvanize the pinned down troops, get them moving and react.

The better organized began to operate in small teams or squads – moving in groups in order to minimize exposure and provide protection.

Heavy machine gun and mortar fire continued to pound the Americans. The Rangers and 116th on Dog White had suffered fifty per cent casualty rates before they even reached the seawall.

Cota had ordered a rifleman to keep German heads down on the bluffs above a spot he had chosen for his assault. He then supervised the use of Bangalore torpedoes to blow barbed wire entanglements to shreds – this worked and gave an opportunity for the first few men to break through and head up the bluffs. However, the very first man through was cut down by machine gun fire, sobbing 'Mama' several times before dying.

Brigadier General Norman D. Cota.

Again, leadership matters.

At that moment, Cota jumped to his feet and rushed the gap in the wire, realizing that if he did not then who else would go next?

They followed and by 0900 Cota had his small group of men on top of the bluffs, organized into fire teams and targeting German machine gun positions.

Given how long it had taken to start to get off the beachhead, there was a severe congestion of men and material and, as the tide started to draw in as the morning progressed at a rate of eighty yards per hour, space on the beach was shrinking by the minute.

Some injured men, unable to move, drowned where they lay.

At 0915, back aboard USS *Augusta*, V Corps Commander Major General Leonard T. Gerow briefed General Omar Bradley on the events unfolding on Omaha. Bradley considered abandoning the beach and sending his remaining forces to Utah or the British beaches instead.

Special Brigade troops, tasked with clearing the beach of obstacles, struggled through the chaos, carnage and rising tide: they suffered forty per cent casualty rates but their bravery was astonishing. In order to destroy many of the structures, a man had to stand on another's shoulders so that they could place their explosive charges alongside the mines atop them. This meant that they were clearly exposed to German guns and goes some way to explaining the high casualty rate.

Easy Green and Easy Red sectors afforded more space but the beach exits were clogged up for some time. Also, not all landings were of the same strength. Dog Green was certainly the worst sector but Dog Red was far less intense.

This brutal, panicked, claustrophobic slaughter continued for an hour and a half before there was any sign that this might be anything but a complete disaster for the Allies in this sector.

Back up on the bluffs, Colonel Canham, who had made it up through the fiercely contested Dog Green sector, met up with General Cota who, having initially assaulted through Dog White, had moved west, heading to Vierville. They agreed to split their forces: Cota headed to clear the D1 Vierville draw whilst Canham took his men east to tackle the D3 les Moulins draw from the rear.

By late morning large navy destroyers managed to get in close to the beach – so close that some captains reported that their keel scraped the sea bed – and began to pound German positions and, once tanks began to mass and bring concentrated fire to bear, the advance gained some traction.

Cota reached the rear of the Vierville draw in the aftermath of this heavy naval bombardment. Cota only had five men with him; but the handful of dazed Germans surrendered to him. Using the Germans to guide him, Cota reached the beach, probably on the dividing line between Charlie and Dog Green, and then set about directing infantry up the bluffs and directing engineers to blow anti-tank barriers. He then moved on to les Moulins to help with the efforts in securing that draw too.

Cota's leadership underlines the importance of individual actions during the chaos of confused fighting. Without him and Canham, it is possible to consider whether a footing on top of the bluffs above Omaha would have been managed at all.

From late morning and through to early afternoon, follow up landings were made and men and material began to make their way off the beach and up onto the bluffs and beyond. Danger did not die away, however: booby traps, minefields and German mortars continued to cause casualties. Doctors on the ships were inundated with casualties brought back from the beaches. Some of these were beyond hope and were simply given morphine to ease their journey into the next world.

Dead bodies were stored in ships' refrigerators for the time being.

Many men lost limbs on the minefields.

By the end of the day the Americans had planned for an 8km penetration inland at Omaha. The advance had slogged its way inland by barely 2.5km. The 29th Division suffered 2,440 casualties and the 1st Division 1,774. It was the deadliest of all the beaches.

It was a dreadful day on this beach. But the landing had been made.

General Gerow had managed to reach the Corps command post ashore by 2030 hours, just in time to keep to his wish to establish his position on French soil by nightfall.

As darkness enveloped the beach the full moon cast a dim light over the bodies on the beach – some stacked in piles, others where they fell.

4. Pointe du Hoc – site, bunkers, Rangers' Memorial

1 hour

Pointe du Hoc Ranger Monument
14450 Cricqueville-en-Bessin
France
tel: +33 (0)2 31 51 62 00
Lat & Long: 49.39468 -0.98900

From the Statue of Peace, Grandcamp-Maisy, continue east on the D514 for 3.2km. At the roundabout take the 2nd exit onto Rue Talbot/D514A. After a few hundred metres you will reach the Pointe du Hoc visitor centre and parking.

Context

A preserved battlefield site with bunkers and a memorial to the action undertaken here by elements of the American Second Ranger Battalion.

Orientation

This was a German artillery position on the top of hundred-foot-high cliffs. It was thought to contain 155mm gun emplacements that would be able to fire on Utah and Omaha Beaches, with potentially devastating consequences for the landing forces there. Utah is to the west of this position (to your left as you stand at the memorial itself, looking out to sea) and Omaha to the right (6.4 km).

Stand somewhere close to the Ranger memorial.

Narrative

This is Pointe du Hoc, the site of a formidable German defensive position that had the potential to severely disrupt the success of the American landings at Omaha and Utah.

On the drive to this site today one leaves the D514 and travels down a smaller road. In 1944 this was not such an easy journey. As the Germans felt that this site was virtually impregnable by sea, the landward side was heavily layered with barbed wire and a well-guarded check-point.

The site itself contained six gun emplacements, which were thought to contain 155mm guns with a range of 20km. It was for this reason that the Americans targeted the position as a strategic target.

Yet they were not going to attack from the landward side. Nor were they going to use airborne troops here.

Men would climb these hundred feet cliffs and assault the German defenders head on. The aim was to neutralize the guns and then secure the position.

Which men?

Rangers.

Two Ranger Battalions (2nd and 5th) were subordinated to the 116th Infantry Regiment as part of the 1st Infantry Division and operating within General Gerow's V Corps.

Three companies of the 2nd Battalion were to carry out the initial assault and, if successful, they would release flares signalling for a second wave (two more companies of the 2nd and the entire 5th Battalion) to follow up.

The position itself had been bombed throughout April and May and was intensively battered just before H-Hour on D-Day.

Lieutenant Colonel James E. Rudder would lead the assault after Major Cleveland A. Lytle, who was supposed to command it, went into an alcohol-fuelled rant about the suicidal nature of the task at hand during a briefing aboard a landing ship and was (unsurprisingly) removed from command. He had heard a rumour from the French Resistance that the guns were not in place. In the midst of the commotion he punched a medical officer and, restrained, was moved to his cabin.

Pointe du Hoc preserved battlefield site.

Part of the bunker and blockhouse network.

Rudder had trained the men; he knew every element of the plan and he knew that what these men needed now, more than anything, was leadership and certainty – panic is a cancer, it spreads and destroys.

The mission began.

Twenty minutes before H-Hour, the twelve landing craft of the initial 2nd Battalion forces approached the Normandy coastline. They were aiming to hit the slither of beach below the cliffs at H-Hour exactly.

88 *Visiting the Normandy Invasion Beaches and Battlefields*

View from an advanced bunker and lookout position.

However, the strong tides began to drag the flotilla east and, to exacerbate matters, Pointe de la Percée, 4.5 kilometres east, was mistaken for Pointe du Hoc by the Royal Navy coxswain.

Rudder realized the mistake and turned the boats around. However, they then sailed parallel to shore, only a hundred yards out to sea and under direct fire from the positions on this cliff.

Forty minutes later than anticipated, Rudder's boat hit the beach first, approximately 600 yards to the right of this position. The Rangers sprinted to the cliff face.

Rocket-fired grappling irons, developed for British Commandos, were utilised in an initial attempt to secure a hold but, heavy with sea water, most struggled to gain any real height. A few did hold and the first Rangers were on their way.

On top of the cliffs there was a mixture of panic and bewilderment. Eighteen bombers had, just twenty minutes ago, targeted the position. In the hours immediately before H-Hour, 14-inch shells fired from USS *Texas* had rained down upon the Germans.

After this onslaught, some of the garrison emerged and quickly saw what was happening below them; grenades were thrown down on to the Rangers. Some of them, reminiscent of siege defence from earlier times, hurled rocks down the cliffs.

However, support fire from the US destroyer *Satterlee* and British destroyer *Talybont* did an effective job of keeping this response pinned down.

Back at the base of the cliffs, Rangers were now using London fire brigade ladders, climbing axes and daggers to inch their way up the rock face. To give a sense of the confusion on the cliff tops, the Germans thought that some type of special shell was being fired from Allied warships from which rope ladders were falling out!

In many places, once the initial forty feet or so of sheer cliff were climbed using the ladders and rope, men could then make the rest of the way by scrambling up on their knees and elbows.

German soldiers ran for cover, scrambled to gun emplacements whilst – bit by bit – Rangers reached the top of the cliff.

German resistance was not strong – again an indication of the poor quality forces in the area – and many of those who had not scrambled into the concrete emplacements melted away into the fields beyond.

At this stage the Rangers were supposed to radio the success signal: 'Praise the Lord'. This would then initiate the second wave assault from the rest of the 2nd and the whole of the 5th Battalion. But the radios were not working – sea water had done its corrosive work.

Eventually a flare was fired.

Too late. Due to the initial delay in landing, the second assault wave had proceeded to its alternative plan: land on Omaha Beach in support of the 116th.[11]

But where were the guns?

The 155mm guns were not in their casemates; indeed, telegraph poles were in situ in some of the emplacements. Yet pre-invasion intelligence had been certain about the weaponry.

Rudder split his forces.

One group stayed and prepared to defend the newly held position, the other set off in search of the heavy guns.

Five of the six guns were eventually located in an orchard at the end of what is now Ranger Road (the road to the Pointe du Hoc complex) off the D514. Using thermite grenades, Sergeant Leonard G. Lomell incapacitated them.

Drunken Major Lytle had been correct.

Where once hell raged, tourists now stroll.

But why were they not in place?

It appears that the Germans removed the guns once the heavy bombing of the position began to take place in April.

Even so, the assault had occurred and now the Rangers had to hold their position whilst waiting for reinforcements and relief.

Later in the day the 914th Grenadier Regiment began a series of heavy counter-attacks. By nightfall the Rangers were barely hanging on to a position just a couple of hundred yards wide at the edge of the cliff.

Yet the Rangers stood fast. They survived heavy machine gun fire originating from the concrete bunker on top of which the memorial now rises and fierce shelling.

The fog, uncertainty and darkness of war certainly emerged during these brutally tough hours for the Rangers. It was reported after the battle by one of the Rangers that a number of French civilians were shot in retribution by the Americans due to the fact that they had been firing at them and acting as artillery observers for the German forces.

During the night of 7 June German forces withdrew and the Rangers were finally relieved by 116th Infantry Regiment and 5th Ranger Battalion at midday on the 8th; but not before four men were killed by shell fire from US Sherman tanks who had been confused by the sound of German guns firing. German guns were, indeed, firing but it was the Rangers who were doing the shooting – they had run out of their own ammunition.

Out of 225 men who undertook the attack, 135 were killed, wounded or missing.

But Pointe du Hoc had been taken.

* * *

Captain Ronald Reagan, serving as part of the First Motion Picture Unit during the Second World War.

On 6 June 1984, to mark forty years since D-Day, US President Ronald Reagan made a speech in front of the Ranger memorial. Addressing world dignitaries and veterans he spoke powerfully of the achievements of D-Day. It is worth considering his fine words at length:

'We're here to mark that day in history when the Allied armies joined in battle to reclaim this continent to liberty. For four long years, much of Europe had been under a terrible shadow. Free nations had fallen, Jews cried out in the camps, millions cried out for liberation. Europe was enslaved, and the world prayed for its rescue. Here in Normandy the rescue began. Here the Allies stood and fought against tyranny in a giant undertaking unparalleled in human history.

We stand on a lonely, windswept point on the northern shore of France. The air is soft, but forty years ago at this moment the air was dense with smoke and the cries of men; and the air was filled with the crack of rifle fire and the roar of cannon. At dawn, on the morning of the 6th of June, 1944, 225 Rangers jumped off the British landing craft and ran to the bottom of these cliffs. Their mission was one of the most difficult and daring of the invasion: to climb these sheer and desolate cliffs and take out the enemy guns. The Allies had been told that some of the mightiest of these guns were here and they would be trained on the beaches to stop the Allied advance.

The Rangers looked up and saw the enemy soldiers [at] the edge of the cliffs shooting down at them with machine guns and throwing grenades. And the American Rangers began to climb. They shot rope ladders over the face of these cliffs and began to pull themselves up. When one Ranger fell, another would take his place. When one rope was cut, a Ranger would grab another and begin his climb again. They climbed, shot back, and held their footing. Soon, one by one, the Rangers pulled themselves over the top and in seizing the firm land at the top of these cliffs they began to seize back the continent of Europe. Two hundred and twenty-five came here. After two days of fighting, only ninety could still bear arms.

Behind me is a memorial that symbolizes the Ranger daggers that were thrust into the top of these cliffs. And before me are the men who put them there.

These are the boys of Pointe du Hoc. These are the men who took the cliffs. These are the champions who helped free a continent. These are the heroes who helped end a war.

Gentlemen, I look at you and I think of the words of Stephen Spender's poem. You are men who in your "lives fought for life . . . and left the vivid air signed with your honor".

Rangers' Memorial.

I think I know what you may be thinking right now – thinking "we were just part of a bigger effort; everyone was brave that day". Well, everyone was. Do you remember the story of Bill Millin[12] of the 51st Highlanders? Forty years ago today, British troops were pinned down near a bridge, waiting desperately for help. Suddenly, they heard the sound of bagpipes, and some thought they were dreaming. Well, they weren't. They looked up and saw Bill Millin with his bagpipes, leading the reinforcements and ignoring the smack of the bullets into the ground around him.

Lord Lovat was with him – Lord Lovat of Scotland, who calmly announced when he got to the bridge, "Sorry I'm a few minutes late," as if he'd been delayed by a traffic jam, when in truth he'd just come from the bloody fighting on Sword Beach, which he and his men had just taken.

There was the impossible valor of the Poles who threw themselves between the enemy and the rest of Europe as the invasion took hold, and the unsurpassed courage of the Canadians who had already seen the horrors of war on this coast. They knew what awaited them there, but they would not be deterred. And once they hit Juno Beach, they never looked back.

All of these men were part of a roll call of honor with names that spoke of a pride as bright as the colors they bore: the Royal Winnipeg Rifles, Poland's 24th Lancers, the Royal Scots Fusiliers, the Screaming Eagles, the Yeomen of England's armored division, the forces of Free France, the Coast Guard's "Matchbox Fleet" and you, the American Rangers.

Forty summers have passed since the battle that you fought here. You were young the day you took these cliffs; some of you were hardly more than boys, with the deepest joys of life before you. Yet, you risked everything here. Why? Why did you do it? What impelled you to put aside the instinct for self-preservation and risk your lives to take these cliffs? What inspired all the men of the armies that met here? We look at you, and somehow we know the answer. It was faith and belief; it was loyalty and love.

The men of Normandy had faith that what they were doing was right, faith that they fought for all humanity, faith that a just God would grant them mercy on this beachhead or on the next. It was the deep knowledge – and pray God we have not lost it – that there is a profound, moral difference between the use of force for liberation and the use of force for conquest. You were here to liberate, not to conquer, and so you and those others did not doubt your cause. And you were right not to doubt.

You all knew that some things are worth dying for. One's country is worth dying for, and democracy is worth dying for, because it's the most deeply honorable form of government ever devised by man. All of you loved liberty. All of you were willing to fight tyranny, and you knew the people of your countries were behind you.

The Americans who fought here that morning knew word of the invasion was spreading through the darkness back home. They fought – or felt in their hearts, though they couldn't know in fact, that in Georgia they were filling the churches at 4 a.m., in Kansas they were kneeling on their porches and praying, and in Philadelphia they were ringing the Liberty Bell.

Something else helped the men of D-day: their rockhard belief that Providence would have a great hand in the events that would unfold here; that God was an ally in this great cause. And so, the night before the invasion, when Colonel Wolverton asked his parachute troops to kneel with him in prayer he told them: "Do not bow your heads, but look up so you can see God and ask His blessing in what we're about to do." Also that night, General Matthew Ridgway on his cot, listening in the darkness for the promise God made to Joshua: "I will not fail thee nor forsake thee."

These are the things that impelled them; these are the things that shaped the unity of the Allies.

When the war was over, there were lives to be rebuilt and governments to be returned to the people. There were nations to be reborn. Above all, there was a new peace to be assured. These were huge and daunting tasks. But the Allies summoned strength from the faith, belief, loyalty, and love of those who fell here. They rebuilt a new Europe together.

[…]

We in America have learned bitter lessons from two World Wars: It is better to be here ready to protect the peace than to take blind shelter across the sea, rushing to respond only after freedom is lost. We've learned that isolationism never was and never will be an acceptable response to tyrannical governments with an expansionist intent.

[…]

Here, in this place where the West held together, let us make a vow to our dead. Let us show them by our actions that we understand what they died for. Let our actions say to them the words for which Matthew Ridgway listened: "I will not fail thee nor forsake thee."

A concrete casemate.

94 *Visiting the Normandy Invasion Beaches and Battlefields*

Strengthened by their courage, heartened by their valor, and borne by their memory, let us continue to stand for the ideals for which they lived and died. Thank you very much, and God bless you all.'[13]

Activities

This is a preserved battlefield and a vast site to explore. Shell craters pock-mark the landscape, observation points and concrete casemates and bunkers can all be visited. A granite dagger obelisk memorial sits atop a German concrete bunker and there are a number of information boards and memorial panels around the site. A visitor centre can also be visited.

5. Dog Green Sector, Omaha Beach

45 minutes

14710 Vierville-sur-Mer, France
Lat & Long: 49.37928 -0.90310

Leave the car park at Pointe du Hoc and head south, back down the D514A. At the roundabout take the 2nd exit, heading east on to Hameau au Guay/D514 and stay on this for 6.8km. Then turn left onto the D517. After 500m there is a car park.

A wonderful statue; part of the National Guard Memorial.

Leave your car and continue on foot down the hill towards the beach. You will see the National Guard Memorial on the WN-72 section of the Atlantic Wall defences in front of you.

Gather there.

Context

Easily accessible section of Omaha Beach and, probably, the most deadly part of it for the American forces landing here due to the strong German positions.

Orientation

The memorial is sited on top of WN-72, an anti-tank bunker. If you stand looking out to sea, then to your immediate right is Dog Green sector and to the left is Charlie sector. The road you have just walked down was the tactically vital D1 beach exit draw.

Narrative

Reacquaint yourself with the Omaha Beach history and the general experience of forces of the 116th Regiment (page 81).

Then:

The 29th Division, who had responsibility for the western part of the Omaha beach landings, was a National Guard division. The National Guard bears similarity to the British Territorial Army tradition and drew troops from specific geographic areas who

Looking out over the infamous Dog Green sector.

A view from the beach at Dog Green towards the bluffs beyond.

joined up, trained, fought and, possibly, died together. The 29th Division had never seen action prior to D-Day.

This is the memorial to the actions of the National Guard. It sits atop WN-72 (*Wiederstandsnest,* or resistance point). Each exit, or draw, from the beaches had two such defensive concrete positions guarding them. This one contained a 50mm and a 75mm gun and, as you can see, enjoyed a terrific view of the beach.

This is sector Dog Green of Omaha Beach. It is where Company A of the 116th Regiment landed on D-Day. If, when thinking about that day, your mind throws up those horrific opening battle scenes from *Saving Private Ryan*, then this is the sector that those scenes most accurately reflect.

First, let us consider the geography and the military necessity of the assault here.

Omaha beach stretches for 10km in a crescent shape and, at low tide, has a long, flat stretch of close to 400 metres. In 1944 the beach had more shingle than it does today and, in this sector, used to have a wooden seawall. Further inland from the seawall was a paved road. The Germans had constructed an anti-tank ditch before a short, flat, swampy area at the foot of the steep bluffs. The only way off was through four draws – these were little more than minor track roads but would be crucial to secure and then improved if the necessary men and material were to be successfully landed over the days ahead.

Just pause for a moment and consider the bluffs that you can see rising from the beach here at Dog Green. Compare them to the topography at Utah and one cannot fail to understand the difference in task faced here. Yes, it is relatively straightforward for a fit young man to scale these features but what looks like a reasonable workout today is a mountain to men under fire, carrying heavy packs and weapons whilst fighting for their lives.

This particular beach was an obvious landing site. For one thing, it is almost ten kilometres wide and the only beach between Arromanches and the River Douve. It would have to be taken on D-Day. If not, the risk to the Americans on Utah and the British at Gold was critical – their flanks would be completely open. Rommel was well aware that if the invasion came in Normandy then this would certainly be one of the beaches attacked. Hence the heavy mining, beach obstacles, strong points and pillboxes. Utah was barren compared to the German defences here.

On Dog Green sector there were six German strongpoints, over a third of the strongpoints on Omaha. The ridges were covered with concealed foxholes in which snipers and machine gun nests hid. Those gunners had detailed fields of fire diagrams hanging on the walls in their bunkers. Trench systems were linked to underground, bricked and concreted command posts. This was, for once, a position that lived up to the moniker of Fortress Europe.

Just take another moment to consider the enfilade possibilities across Omaha. Standing at this German gun position, one can see just how exceptional a view they had.

So, what made the Allies think that they could take this beach? To be blunt, not everyone thought they could. Much faith had been put in the pre-landing aerial bombing and follow-up naval gun shelling, combined with the planned 40,000 troops to be landed against an anticipated enemy force of 800 *Osttruppen*.

What actually happened was that the air raids hit positions too far inland, the naval bombardment was nowhere near concentrated enough, the defenders here were mainly from the good quality 352nd Division (about whose presence the Allies had no idea) and there were far more than 800 of them.

Company A of the 116th Regiment were the only unit to land accurately on Omaha. They hit Dog Green. This is what happened to them.

Approximately sixty per cent of Company A were from the town of Bedford, Virginia. Much like the impact of the devastation of the Pals Battalions on 1 July 1916, the concentration of loss from such a small locality would bring sad consequences for the community.

They landed opposite the Vierville draw and, crucially, were an isolated group. G and F Companies should have been beside them but, due to the weather and the fog of war, they had drifted a kilometre further east.

Therefore, when those ramps dropped, the heavily manned German positions opposite Company A concentrated their hellish fire upon those men.

The effect was utterly dreadful.

Of the 200 or so men who landed with Company A on D-Day, fewer than thirty survived.

The stories of their experiences are horrific. Lieutenant Edward Tidrick left his boat and was immediately hit in the throat. Staggering on forward, he fell to his knees and urged those around him to 'Advance with the wire cutters!'. Machine gun bullets tore through him from head to waist.

On one landing craft, every man of the thirty-strong cargo was killed before exiting the boat.

Men became entwined in their own personal struggle with death; many drowned as they desperately tried to get ashore whilst under fire.

One landing craft was annihilated by four direct mortar hits.

Men soon lost order as they scrambled for cover – and some, unable to find any, then ran back to the sea to try to locate some sort of protection.

By 0640 only one officer remained alive and he, Lieutenant E. Ray Nance, was badly wounded.

Within fifteen minutes of landing, Company A was effectively utterly destroyed. Those who were badly injured simply lay where they were. The few survivors huddled against the sea wall.

The regimental history states that, 'Company A ceased to be an assault company and had become a forlorn little rescue party bent on survival and the saving of the lives of other men.'

Yet they had landed and their losses were not in vain. Their weapons, light and heavy, were ashore. Follow up waves would relieve them and, literally, pick up these weapons and take the Allied assault inland.

When stood on the beach today, it is impossible for us to comprehend what once took place here. Yet it did. By being here we remember each individual and their actions, even if the detail is lost to history.

It is appropriate and common to be swept away with melancholy at this most blood-stained of places. However, it can bring some comfort, and perhaps a fleeting smile to one's face, to remember one of the more colourful of pre-invasion rallying calls from a certain US General:

> 'There is one great thing that you men will all be able to say after this war is over and you are home once again. You may be thankful that twenty years from now when you are sitting by the fireplace with your grandson on your knee and he asks you what you did in the great World War II, you won't have to cough, shift him to the other knee and say, Well, your Granddaddy shovelled shit in Louisiana.'
>
> General George S. Patton, Jr (the speech was delivered to Patton's troops on 5 June, 1944).

The National Guard Memorial.

Why was Omaha so bloody in comparison to the other beaches? It is true that the Americans had not made use of the specialist equipment that the British would, notably 'Hobart's Funnies' tanks. British engineers landed simultaneously with armoured support on their beach sections and the Americans did not do this.

However, simply to stand on Omaha and look at the bluffs ahead, the field of fire available to the Germans and the sheer size of the beach to be crossed is enough to understand the task that they faced.

What did it cost to take Omaha?

Blood.

Activities

Lots to look at: the National Guard memorial contains information relating to the Guard's history. Below the memorial is a German bunker and remains of the American Mulberry Harbour which was destroyed due to a huge storm on 19 June. It is also a very sobering moment, tide permitting, to walk down on to Dog Green Sector and look up at the bluffs from beach level. You can also see, and walk to if you wish, further German bunker positions on the bluffs to the right (if you are on the beach looking back up at land).

This is certainly one of those 'walking in the footsteps of history' moments. It can hit one, as it were, right between the eyes.

6. The Normandy American Cemetery and Memorial

1–3 hours

Normandy American Cemetery
American Cemetery
14710
Colleville-sur-Mer
France
tel Phone: +33 (0)2 31 51 62 00
Lat & Long: 49.35658 -0.85297

Leave the car park in Vierville-sur-Mer and head south-west on the D517 towards Route de Grandcamp/D514. Turn left onto the Route de Grandcamp/D514 and continue for 5km. At the roundabout take the 3rd exit and follow the signs for parking at the site.

Context

A cemetery and memorial to American troops.

This is a vast site with much to see, both in the cemetery and from the beach below.

Narrative

There are 9,387 burials in this cemetery which is a fitting resting place for many of those from the United States of America who lost their lives in the liberation of Europe.

If you have ever visited Washington DC then you will not fail to recognize similarities in the neo-classical style and sheer scale of this striking and emotive place.

Amongst the buried here are three Medal of Honor winners and two of the Niland brothers, whose story inspired the film *Saving Private Ryan*, the opening scenes of which were filmed here.

There is a memorial to 1,557 Americans who lost their lives and have no known grave. Their names are inscribed on the walls of a semicircular garden. A reflective pool shimmers in front whilst *The Spirit of American Youth Rising from the Waves*, a 22-foot bronze statue, towers above. The two American flags are raised each morning and lowered every evening.

The memorial is designed to face the United States at its nearest point to the cemetery; this would be between Eastport and Lubec, Maine, New England.

An excellent visitor centre tells the stories of individuals who took part in the Normandy campaign and there is also a chapel at the heart of the cemetery.

And, perhaps most importantly, the cemetery is sited on top of the bluffs above Omaha Beach on which many men, buried here, lost their lives.

Notable burials:

Lesley J. McNair, US Army lieutenant general, promoted to general posthumously: one of the four highest-ranking Americans to be killed in action in World War II. He was renowned for his training of troops for combat and is recognized as one of the most important individuals in preparing American forces for realistic combat situations. He was killed on 25 July 1944 by friendly fire aerial bombing.

Plot F, Row 28, Grave 42

Jimmie W. Monteith: Medal of Honor recipient.

His citation:

'For conspicuous gallantry and intrepidity above and beyond the call of duty on 6 June 1944, while serving with 16th Infantry Regiment, 1st Infantry Division, in action near Colleville-sur-Mer, France. First Lieutenant Monteith landed with the initial assault waves on the coast of France under heavy enemy fire. Without regard to his own personal safety he continually moved up and down the beach, reorganizing men for further assault. He then led the assault over a narrow protective ledge and across the flat, exposed terrain to the comparative safety of a cliff. Retracing his steps across the field to the beach, he moved over to where two tanks were buttoned up and blind under violent enemy artillery and machine gun fire. Completely exposed to the intense fire, First Lieutenant Monteith led the tanks on foot through a minefield and into firing positions. Under his direction several enemy positions were destroyed. He then rejoined his company and under his leadership his men captured an advantageous position on the hill. Supervising the defense of his newly won position against repeated vicious counterattacks, he continued to ignore his own personal safety, repeatedly crossing the 200 or 300 yards of open terrain under heavy fire to strengthen links in his defensive chain. When the enemy succeeded in completely surrounding First Lieutenant Monteith and his unit and while leading the fight out of the situation, First Lieutenant Monteith was killed by enemy fire. The courage, gallantry and intrepid leadership displayed by First Lieutenant Monteith is worthy of emulation.'

Plot I, row 20, grave 12

Two of the Niland brothers: Preston and Robert

Preston Niland was killed on 7 June near Utah Beach whilst his brother, Robert, a member of the 82nd Airborne, was killed the previous day when holding off a German advance whilst his company retreated.

The link to the film *Saving Private Ryan* is that another brother, Edward, was also thought to be dead, killed in action in Burma, whilst the fourth brother, Frederick 'Fritz' was part of 101st Airborne Easy Company and had also taken part in the D-Day landings. Given the apparent loss of three brothers, Fritz was brought out of the line of fire and, eventually, back to America. In the fictional film, Private James Ryan is loosely based on Fritz. In a positive twist, Edward Nilan was not actually killed but was held in a Japanese Prisoner of War camp until he was liberated on 4 May, 1945.

Preston: Plot F, Row 15, Grave 12
Robert: Plot F, Row 15, Grave 11

Frank D. Peregory: Medal of Honor recipient (see page 79)

Plot G, row 21, grave 7

Theodore Roosevelt, Jr.: son of President Theodore Roosevelt, Medal of Honor recipient (see pages 72 and 74)

Citation:

'For gallantry and intrepidity at the risk of his life above and beyond the call of duty on 6 June 1944, in France. After 2 verbal requests to accompany the leading assault elements in the Normandy invasion had been denied, Brig. Gen. Roosevelt's written request for this mission was approved and he landed with the first wave of the forces assaulting the enemy-held beaches. He repeatedly led groups from the beach, over the seawall and established them inland. His valor, courage, and presence in the very front of the attack and his complete unconcern at being under heavy fire inspired the troops to heights of enthusiasm and self-sacrifice. Although the enemy had the beach under constant direct fire, Brig. Gen. Roosevelt moved from one locality to another, rallying men around him, directed and personally led them against the enemy. Under his seasoned, precise, calm and unfaltering leadership, assault troops reduced beach strong points and rapidly moved inland with minimum casualties. He thus contributed substantially to the successful establishment of the beachhead in France.'

Plot D, Row 28, Grave 45

Quentin Roosevelt: son of President Theodore Roosevelt, aviator killed in action in World War I

Quentin died in aerial combat during the Great War but, in 1955, his remains were reinterred here so that he would forever lie next to his older brother.

Plot D, Row 28, Grave 46

This is a very special place and one that very few will ever forget after they have visited.

A fitting end to a day dedicated to the actions of American forces on D-Day.

Activities

Walk the cemetery and take in the sheer scale. There are two very good battle maps in the memorial that deserve study and one should really make the time to walk down to the beach, accessible from the cemetery, and look back up at the bluffs above – again, a very sobering moment.

* * *

– DAY END –

Footnotes:

1. These timings are a rough guide and do not include any travel between stops. Always keep in mind just how long it takes to get groups off and on coaches.
2. These instructions assume that you are 'guiding' a group. If you are not then these work as suggestions of which areas of the book you might wish to re-visit at a given site.
3. Actually, many Austrian soldiers were stationed here and were quick to abandon their positions in the hours ahead.
4. Opposite the church, roughly where the museum now stands.
5. His son, Captain Quentin Roosevelt II, landed at Omaha Beach on D-Day. Unfortunately Theodore Roosevelt Jr would die of a heart attack on July 12 and never lived to know that Eisenhower had that same day approved his promotion to major general. He is buried in the Normandy American Cemetery.
6. David was the Lieutenant Governor of Texas from 2003–2015. Both he and Eugene are highly successful businessmen.
7. Technical Sergeant – known as Sergeant First Class since 1948.
8. One humorous (though I am sure not for the men involved) occurrence that happened to a group of 29th Infantry Division on D-Day was when their assault craft was being lowered from HMS *Empire Javelin*. The mechanism lowering the craft jammed and the men were stuck dangling in their craft for 30 minutes. Not only that but they were stuck right under the ship's heads (toilets). Major Dallas noted that the men 'made the most of an opportunity which Englishmen have sought since 1776'. One 'survivor' of the ordeal said that 'We cursed, we cried and we laughed […] When we started for shore, we were all covered with shit.'

9. This overestimation of the German Omaha Beach defensive forces is a common error in many publications.
10. This is an interesting phenomenon that is reported by survivors of extremely distressing situations such as terror attacks or major accidents. The science is not conclusive yet but can be placed, very roughly, into two camps: 1) your brain is working at a quicker rate in an attempt to help you survive the situation (i.e. finding solutions/reacting rapidly) and thus it seems as though time slows down because you are functioning at an increased pace. Or 2) it is a memory trick. Due to the rich and deep experience that you have encountered, it is when you recall it afterwards that time seems to have slowed but, in fact, it is simply because you remember more of it and in vivid detail.
11. Although this made it far more difficult for the Rangers to hold Pointe du Hoc, it may have inadvertently led to success at Omaha. The addition of 500 Rangers, under the command of Brigadier General Cota, assaulting the bluffs at Omaha perhaps tilted the battle decisively in favour of the Americans on that beach.
12. See page 129.
13. President Ronald Reagan – 6 June 1984. Ronald Reagan Presidential Library: https://reaganlibrary.archives.gov/archives/speeches/major.html#.V1mawsv2bIV

Tour Two

Sword, Juno and Gold

Two-Day Itinerary

Approximate start time of 0900 and end time of 1600.

To get to all of these sites in one day is possible but not advisable in order to do them justice. Therefore, this is a tour that is best approached over two days and using the additional stops.

All those sites given a letter addition (i.e. 2a, 2b) are, although highly recommended visits, those stops that I would suggest better to leave out if time becomes an issue. If you only have one day then stick to the main stops.

If you would rather take a more leisurely pace and prepare a lighter schedule, then you might plan to visit only the main stops over two days (i.e. 1,2,3...) and if you find that you could do with adding another stop or two along the way then bring in the lettered stop closest to your current location (i.e. if you have just visited 2 then go to 2a). Furthermore, you can look for a museum to add to the schedule (see Museums chapter) and, for additional visits, in order to extend the tour over more days, also see the 'Going further, doing more' chapter.

1. **Merville Battery**

2. **Pegasus Bridge**
    2a. Memorial Pegasus Museum
    2b. General Montgomery Monument, Colleville-Montgomery
    2c. Piper Bill Millin Memorial Statue, Sword Beach

3. **Bény-Sur-Mer Canadian CMWG Cemetery**

4. **Juno Beach**
    4a. Juno Beach Centre

5. **Gold Beach, King Sector, Stan Hollis V.C**
    5a. King Sector

6. **Asnelles, Gold Beach, Jig Sector**
    6a. Arromanches 360°
    6b. Longues Battery

7. **Bayeux CWGC Cemetery**

– TOUR END –

British Army Operations on D-Day

The British Second Army, under the command of the incisive, talented and admirably reserved Lieutenant General Miles Dempsey, was tasked with the responsibility of the Anglo-Canadian beach landings on D-Day.

The width of the assault sector ran to almost forty kilometres. It began from Port-en-Bessin, adjacent to the Americans at Omaha, and ran eastwards along the coastline and through Arromanches, Courseulles, Ouistreham, across the Caen Canal and River Orne before eventually ending at Cabourg and the flooded estuary of the River Dives.

Three beaches offered appropriate landing positions for the troops. The sections of the beaches chosen were each approximately three kilometres long and with very gentle inclines running up to fortified former holiday hamlets and villages. Their codenames: Gold, Juno and Sword.

Gold Beach linked the British to the Americans at Omaha and was the middle assault sector of the whole Overlord plan. XXX Corps, under General Gerard C. Bucknall and led by the 50th (Northumbrian) Division, would carry out the assault, with the main aim being the town of Bayeux, some eight kilometres inland.

Heading eastwards, Juno Beach was the target of I Corps, with the 3rd Canadian Division leading. One of the aims of this landing was to ensure the link between Gold and Sword beach.

Sword beach was the most easterly assault beach on D-Day and also came under the command of I Corps. 3rd (British) Division had to secure this sector, with the city of Caen, twelve kilometres inland, being a first day objective. Montgomery intended to draw German reinforcements into a fight around Caen before the real Allied breakout would occur on the western flank of the invasion, with the American forces eventually pivoting back to link up with the British and drive the Germans back.[1]

However, that eastern flank at Sword was extremely vulnerable: firstly, the 125th Regiment of 21st Panzer Division was stationed near Caen and had the potential to react with pace and throw the British back into the sea;[2] second, bridges over the flooded River Dives were routes from which German reinforcements could counter-attack in the days ahead; third, the two bridges at Bénouville across the Caen Canal and River Orne were the only two between Caen and the sea and thus control of them was vital; fourth, a German artillery battery near Merville could cause severe damage to the landings at Sword. The final two points are important when considered together. Any troops used to neutralise the Merville Battery would need the bridges to be intact if they were not to be cut off from the rest of the assault at Sword.

Who would be ordered to carry out both of these critical tasks?

6th Airborne Division.

British Airborne Operations on D-Day

The British air assault would be carried out by the 6th Airborne Division, led by the colourful, characterful and inspirational Major General Richard 'Windy' Gale.

Gale, like most of the senior commanders on D-Day, was a veteran of the Great War. After his experiences of that war he became sceptical of the value of heavy firepower dominated operations and learnt some invaluable lessons from the fighting that was

Binocular-clad, cigarette in hand, Major General Richard 'Windy' Gale.

emerging in 1918: lightly armed, well-trained forces moving at speed and utilising surprise could achieve impressive victories.

Gale theorised that developing elite forces who could use shock and awe, movement and surprise was just as important as the number of troops that you had at your disposal.

In 1941 the British Army expanded its airborne forces and Gale was given command of the new 1st Parachute Brigade. Starting with a blank canvas, Gale made key appointments and then devised the training regimes from scratch. He was then appointed Director of Air at the War Office, where he had the unenviable task of trying to solve inter-service rivalry between the RAF and Army over the use of aircraft – the RAF were reticent in providing aircraft to the Army for airborne assaults, instead promoting the superiority of aerial bombardment as a war-winning method.

Crucially, in 1943 Gale was promoted to major general and given command of the new 6th Airborne Division. It contained two parachute brigades, made up of battalions from the Parachute Regiment, and one air landing brigade, comprising infantry soldiers who would land via glider. This Division had been given the task of carrying out Operation Tonga – the airborne landings as part of Overlord. He had under a year to train his men for what would be a crucial element of D-Day.

The results were breathtaking.

* * *

On D-Day the 6th Airborne Division plan was to land on the most eastern flank of the entire operation, adjacent to the operations at Sword.

The objectives: capture and hold the bridges over the Caen Canal and River Orne; neutralise the Merville Battery; destroy the bridges over the flooded River Dives in order to limit German counterattacks; secure the flank of the invasion area.

There were nine Drop or Landing Zones[3] for an operation executed in three phases. The *coup de main*[4] operation was the assault on the Caen Canal and River Orne bridges; this began when the first glider hit the ground at 0016 hours on D-Day.

Gale, in contrast to his American Airborne counterparts, had trained his men to work in small commando-style units with limited but highly specific objectives. Applying his theories and lessons of war, Gale intended to use the cover of darkness in a challenging early hours assault in order to heighten the element of surprise and thus increase the chances of success.

The capture of the bridges was carried off with a stunning assault that lasted little more than ten minutes. Attempted counter-attacks were successfully repulsed. In the following hour, paratroopers of the 5th Parachute Brigade began to arrive. The assault on Merville Battery did not go smoothly but, despite the difficulties faced, it was neutralised before H-Hour. Men from the 3rd Parachute Brigade had managed to destroy the bridges over the River Dives and securing the flank was well underway. Gale himself was on the ground, following a glider landing a little before 0400 hours.

As daylight broke, the next phase of the airborne drops could take place as gliders brought in reinforcements and supplies. At around midday, airborne troops on the Canal and Orne bridges heard the sound of bagpipes, signalling the arrival of Lord Lovat's 1st Special Service (Commando) Brigade, following their successful landing at Sword Beach. Thus, airborne had linked up with the main invasion troops.

Of course not everything ran smoothly. As will be discussed, the Merville Battery operation came close to disaster. Out of ninety-eight gliders, twenty-two did not make their landing zones due to malfunctions or landing in the wrong place and 71 of the 196 Glider Pilot Regiment troops were casualties.

However, it is clear that Gale's belief in elite forces, intense training, surprise and movement had been delivered with aplomb.

1. Merville Battery

1 hour

Merville is a small town, west of Cabourg. It can be reached by leaving the D514 as you pass through Franceville-Plage and taking Avenue de la Hogue du Moulin. This then becomes the Avenue Alexandre de Lavergne. A right turning on to Avenue de la Batterie de Merville will bring you to the site; but it is a well signposted and advertised location which you should have little difficulty in locating once in the vicinity.

Place du 9ème Bataillon,
14810 Merville-Franceville-Plage,
France.
Tel: +33 2 31 91 47 53
www.batterie-merville.com
Lat & Long: 49.27020 -0.19654

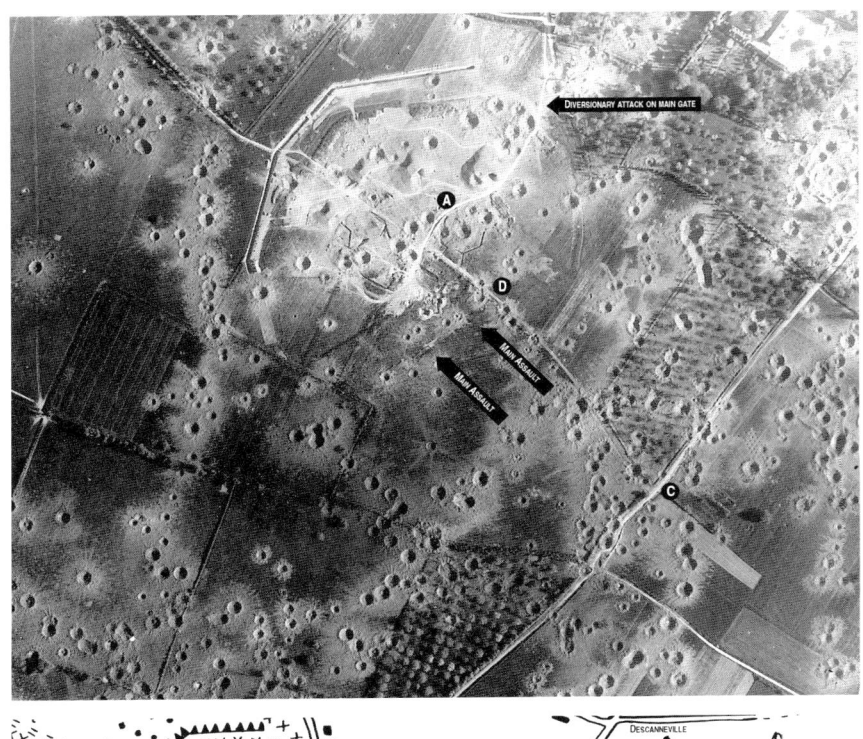

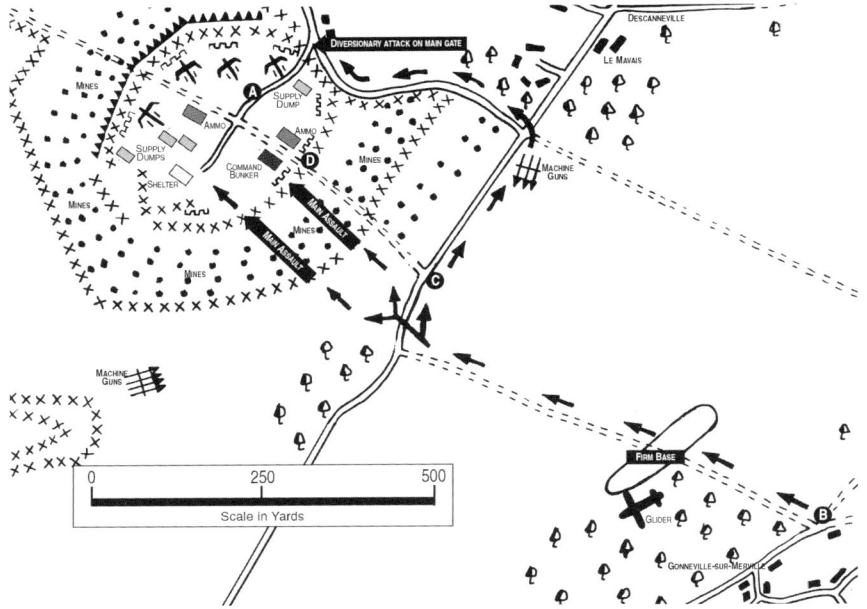

110 *Visiting the Normandy Invasion Beaches and Battlefields*

Key:
A – opposite the second casemate
B – crossroads where Lt Col Otway met up with his reconnaissance
  party and then began the advance on the battery
C – corner of the track leading back into the battery
D – concrete platform: top of the ammunition shelter

Context

A German field gun battery site consisting of four concrete gun casemates. Elements of the Airborne Division were tasked with neutralising this position prior to H-Hour so that it could not disrupt the landings on Sword Beach.

Orientation

Helpfully, the C-47 Dakota on the site is pointing north-west towards Sword Beach, approximately 6km away.

Narrative

Intelligence reports prior to D-Day estimated that there were approximately 200 men garrisoned here at the Merville Battery site. It was a well defended part of the Atlantic Wall system, with rings of barbed wire and minefield perimeters, two flak guns and twelve machine guns. However, the crucial detail and what concerned those planning the beach landings were the four concrete gun casemates. It was believed that these held powerful 155mm howitzer guns that could ravage Sword Beach and disrupt the operation throughout that area.[5] Therefore, nullifying this threat was deemed crucial and it had to happen before H-Hour.

The 9th Battalion Parachute Regiment of the 3rd Parachute Brigade, 6th Airborne Division, was tasked with this mission. They were commanded by twenty-nine-year-old Lieutenant Colonel Terence Otway.

Otway was renowned for setting high expectations for his men and in demanding that they behave to the highest standards of conduct at all times. Famously, he once arranged for thirty women from the Women's Auxiliary Air Force to visit the pubs near where his men were training in England and use their charms to attempt to entice information from them about their upcoming mission. Not one of the men succumbed!

Making full use of reports from the French Resistance and aerial reconnaissance, a full scale mock-up of the Merville Battery had been built near West Woodhay, Berkshire. For several weeks Otway had been studying it and training his men there.

The plan was good and it had to be: Otway's men were to drop at 0410 and signal, using flares, by 0515 that the mission was a success. If the flares did not go off, then Royal Navy ships would begin heavy shelling of the site.

At 2300 hours on 5 June Otway was making final preparations for the upcoming assault and, no doubt, thinking through every

Lieutenant Colonel Terence Otway.

last detail once again. In his kit bag he had a little extra weight – a bottle of whisky. His men had been prohibited from alcohol in the run up to D-Day; tonight they would get a little snifter to get their blood pumping.

Otway had decided to attack from the south. First, one hundred Lancaster bombers would assault the Battery from above. Three Horsa gliders[6] would land directly within the perimeter of the Battery whilst Otway would lead the rest of the battalion from a holding position in the south. Over thirty Dakota planes would drop the men, heavy gear and weaponry on this position a few hours before the attack. Whilst a diversionary assault took place at the main entrance gate, Bangalore torpedoes would be placed under the barbed wire and engineers would attempt to neutralise the minefields. All things going well, when the gliders came in to land at 0430 the Bangalores would be blown and hundreds of men would flood the German position.

All things did not go well.

To begin with, the Lancaster Bombers failed to land a single bomb on the Merville Battery position – the pre-bombing markers had been put in the wrong place. Otway was not to know, but the very first thing that could go wrong had done so.

Just before 0100, Otway was standing in the doorway of his Dakota, waiting to jump, whisky bottle still in hand but now half-empty. He passed the bottle to a crew member and made his leap into the dark sky and D-Day proper.

He knew the territory into which he was descending in fine detail and, therefore, once the ground below him became clear, he knew that he was heading straight for a farmhouse that held a German battalion headquarters.

He slammed into the wall, quickly released his harness and took a moment to catch his breath.

He was unaware of a window opening nearby.

A German soldier peered out into the darkness … but, a second later, he recoiled back inside as a brick rocketed into his face! One of Otway's men had also landed at the farmhouse and his quick thinking gave the two men a chance to get out of the predicament before they could be captured… or worse.

Otway headed for the rendezvous point: a small wood, east of the Battery.

Upon arrival at the wood, Otway sensed all was not as it should be. Where was everyone? The 9th Battalion was planning to put close to 750 men into this operation – fifty in the glider assault, but the rest should have been at the rendezvous.

Otway could only see a few dozen.

At that moment, Otway's second-in-command, Major Eddie Charlton, greeted him: 'Thank God you've come, sir. The drop's bloody chaos. There's hardly anyone here.' Otway's batman,[7] Joe Wilson, who had also made the rendezvous, told Otway 'I believe sir, you have only got fifty men.' Otway was dejected; his plan seemingly in tatters. Wilson held up a flask – 'shall we take our whisky now sir?' Otway had always built an extra fifteen minutes into his schedule, just in case of a problem. He decided to take those fifteen minutes in the hope that more men and resources would arrive.

But what had happened to the drops?

The Dakotas that carried the Battalion across the Channel had come under sustained fire over France. The planes were also from a recently formed RAF group with very inexperienced pilots and crews. They flew in a loose formation and took their lead from the plane in front – thus if that aircraft released its stick at the wrong time or place then those behind would inevitably follow. The flak fire from below had pushed some of the pilots off course. Others were confused by a strong easterly wind which was whipping up a dust cloud caused by the Lancasters' previous bombing. Some navigators simply made a mistake and mistook the River Dives for the River Orne and thus dropped their stick in the wrong location entirely.

Some men were dropped thirty miles from where they should have been. It took one man four days to get to the battalion. A drop that should have been contained within one mile by half a mile was spread out over fifty square miles. 192 men lost their lives – likely drowned in flooded marshland or in the sea.

In the fifteen minutes' waiting time more men made it to the rendezvous. Otway now had 150 soldiers – less than 25 per cent of his expected number. They had no working radio sets and no engineers. There were no 3-inch mortars and the transport gliders had not arrived and therefore no heavy equipment or vehicles were at their disposal either. He had no doctors.

They did have six conscientious objector medical orderlies.
They did have Bangalore torpedoes.
They had one Vickers machine gun.
They had one carrier pigeon.
Otway turned to his batman: 'What the hell am I going to do, Wilson?'
The reply: 'Only one thing you can do, sir, no need to ask me.'
Otway rallied his men and at 0250 they set out for the Battery. En route they met Major Smith, who had led a reconnaissance team to assess the site – he reassured Otway that there was nothing to cause undue concern.

Two men were sent up ahead. Their jobs were to get close to the wire and listen to any German chatter whilst watching for guard movements. They then crawled through the minefield, clearing a route using their hands to move and defuse as many mines as they could.

At 0420 Otway gathered his men 500 yards from the Battery and divided them into four assault groups.

They were spotted by a German machine gun crew outside the perimeter, who began to fire on their position. Otway despatched a group to neutralise them.

They then waited for a glider assault to come in and start the show…

At 0430, right on time, a glider was spotted overhead. It was also spotted by a German anti-aircraft gun crew who opened fire, hitting the glider in the tail and forcing it to crash land a hundred yards away.

Where were the other two? No time for that, Otway had to react.[8]
The Bangalore torpedoes were detonated, clearing two pathways through the wire.
A small group opened fire at the entrance to cause a diversion.
'Get in, get in!' Otway barked… this assault, against all the odds, was now under way.
The men flooded in through the gaps, Sten guns firing; some men were tasked with pinning down and then neutralising the Germans in the machine gun pits and others headed straight for the casemates in order to disarm the guns.

The fighting was intense, disorientating and tough – the Germans fought hard. Yet within fifteen minutes the Merville Battery was under the control of Otway and his men. 200 German soldiers were killed and twenty-two captured.[9]

Otway, waiting at a gap in the perimeter wire for news of progress, was met by Lieutenant Mike Dowling: 'Battery taken as ordered, sir.'

But had the guns been destroyed? Dowling thought so. Otway sent him back to check – en route he was killed by mortar fire.

Otway went in with a small group of troops to mop up any last resistance and check on the guns. It was at this stage that they realised the guns were not of the calibre previously thought. However, lacking any specialist equipment, it was proving a challenge to destroy them. The breech blocks were removed – this was the best that they could do.

The next task was to get a signal to the Navy before 0530, when HMS *Arethusa* was due to open up her guns.

Again improvising, Otway set off a yellow signal flare which was spotted by an RAF plane above. Lieutenant Jimmy Loring then produced his carrier pigeon from his Denison smock. A message was tied to its leg and then released.

After this, the position came under heavy fire from German artillery, clearly aware that the Battery had been captured and quite clearly unconcerned about any German prisoners.

Otway took his men out of the Battery and to the rendezvous point at Calvary Cross.

At this stage Otway assessed the state of his battalion. Out of 750 men, only 150 had taken part in the action. Of that 150, seventy five were now dead, injured or missing.

From a hopeless position, somehow Otway and his men had succeeded. Adaptation and reaction to events as they unfold is a sign of outstanding leadership; Otway clearly displayed that.

However, this being D-Day, their jobs were not yet over. Otway grouped his men together and they set off for their next objective.

The fight for Merville Battery was not yet finished. Within hours, the Germans had retaken the site and began to repair the guns. On 7 June a British Commando raid retook the position but were then ejected later in the day. Merville Battery would remain under German control for many weeks ahead.

In 1993 Otway travelled back to Merville and met the German commander of the battery. He admitted that he did not have the guts to refuse his handshake. The thought of his men, shot by the Germans as they hung helplessly, their parachutes caught in the trees, still pained him greatly. He did, however, admonish picknickers at the battery, stating that 'I don't like people eating and drinking where my men died'.

In 1997 he unveiled a bronze bust of himself at the Merville Battery.

In 2001 he was awarded the Legion d'Honneur.

Activities

The casemates act as the museum with a different theme in each. There are also many excellent information boards, a C-47 and a sound and light experience.

Key:

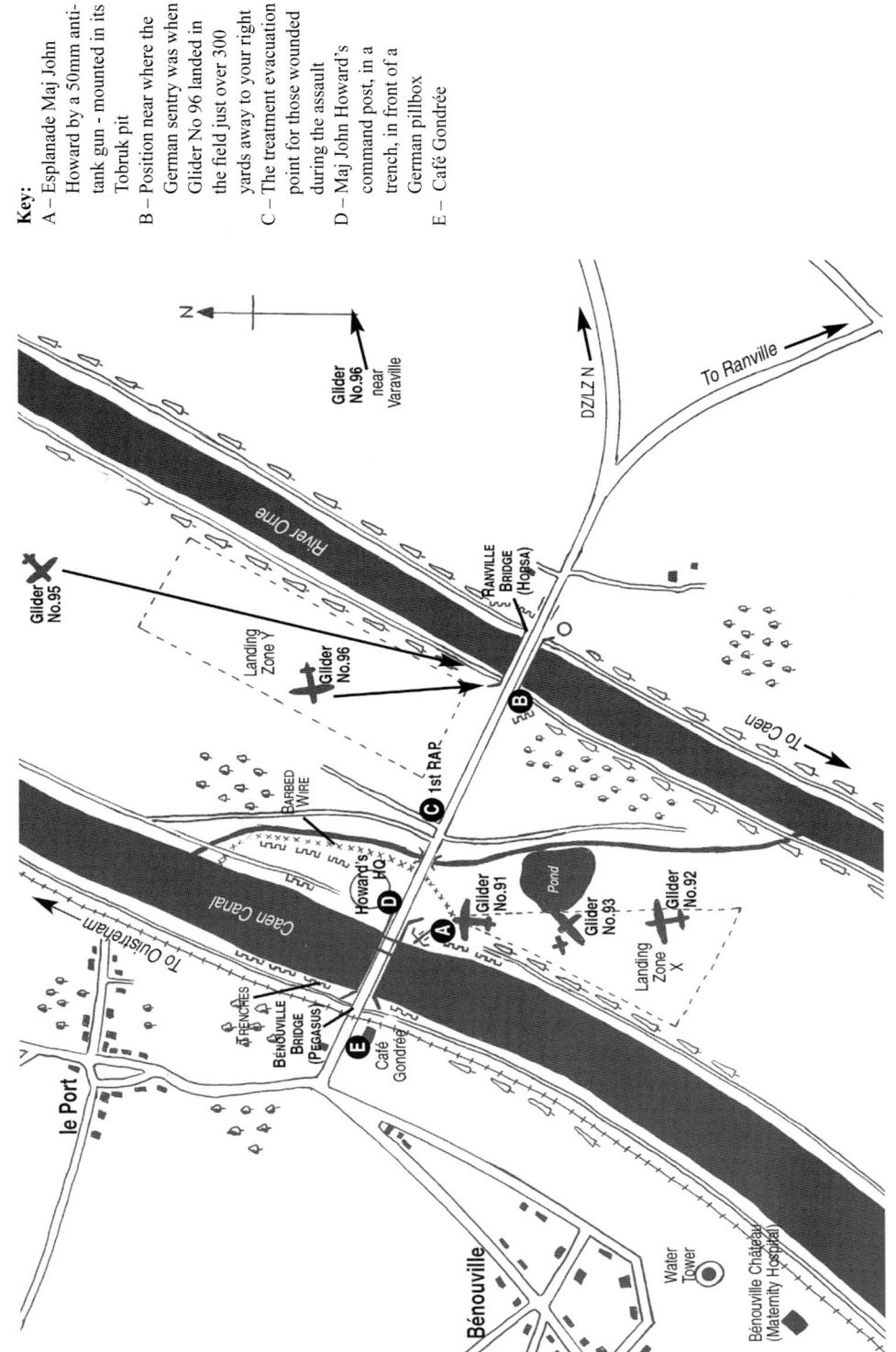

A – Esplanade Maj John Howard by a 50mm anti-tank gun - mounted in its Tobruk pit
B – Position near where the German sentry was when Glider No 96 landed in the field just over 300 yards away to your right
C – The treatment evacuation point for those wounded during the assault
D – Maj John Howard's command post, in a trench, in front of a German pillbox
E – Café Gondrée

The Pegasus Bridge assault area and action mapping.

116 *Visiting the Normandy Invasion Beaches and Battlefields*

2. Pegasus Bridge

45 minutes

Leave the Merville Battery site, joining back up with the Avenue Alexandre de Lavergne and eventually turn left on to the D514. Stay on this towards Bénouville for 7.8km and you will come to the Bridge itself. Car parking is available on Rue Major John Howard, just past the museum. If you are intending to visit the museum, then it has its own carpark.

Lat & Long: 49.2426 -0.2751

Context

Scene of the British Airborne *coup de main* mission on D-Day.

Orientation

Standing on the museum side of the canal, you will see Café Gondrée on the other side. Whilst looking in that direction, the site of the glider landings is immediately to your left, marked by memorial stones with information bronzes. The gliders came in overhead from the north before looping back in from the south to land.

Narrative

Bénouville is a small village but one which had great importance to the success, or not, of Allied operations on D-Day. There are two bridges in close proximity to each other that both traverse stretches of water. The first crossed over the Orne River (Ranville Bridge) and the second over the Caen Canal (Bénouville Bridge) – the latter we now

The Pegasus Bridge site.

Sword, Juno and Gold 117

know as Pegasus Bridge and the former, Horsa Bridge, renamed in honour of the Airborne Division's heroic actions.

Capturing these bridges intact was vital: first, to make Allied troop link-ups across the River and Canal easier but also, much more importantly, to hold back any enemy reinforcements coming from the area of Calais.

In late 1943 Major General Gale decided on a *coup de main* operation, carried out by glider, so that the attacking force could land virtually on top of the German garrison stationed there. If it were to be successful then it would have to be carried out with extreme alacrity.

The Germans had been at the site since 1940 but had been doing much by the way of strengthening the position in 1944: trenches were dug, a 50mm gun added, more barbed wire and roadblocks erected and the siting of a number of anti-glider poles had all taken place. However, as we have previously noted, the quality of the troops in the area was poor and intelligence assessments reckoned on the troops in Bénouville being particularly low quality *Osttruppen* forces.

Major John Howard.

Gale selected the 2nd Battalion Oxfordshire and Buckinghamshire Light Infantry for the operation. The commanding officer, Lieutenant Colonel Roberts, chose D Company for the *coup de main* element, in particular because of the sheer military brilliance of its company commander, Major John Howard.

Howard, a former regular soldier and policeman, was called back into the army at the outbreak of the war. A good indicator of the talents that this remarkable man possessed is the rapidity of his rise from corporal to regimental sergeant major in the King's Shropshire Light Infantry before gaining a commission as an officer and transferring to the Ox & Bucks. By May 1942 he had been given command of D Company in the new 1st Airlanding Brigade.

Howard was a man who took his duties seriously; a person of unwavering solidity and calm yet, by his own admission, a sentimental and deeply caring individual. He was, in many ways, the ideal man to lead such a daring undertaking.

Howard was informed of his mission in April 1944 and the following month he led his men through a preparatory exercise named Operation Mush, using men of the 1st Polish Parachute Brigade as the 'enemy'. When, at the end of the exercise, it was ruled that D Company had not captured the bridges and had, in fact, effectively destroyed one of its own platoons, this highlighted the difficulties that Howard's men would face making a night attack. In the weeks that followed, Howard drilled his men time and again on the art of bridge capture. His men did not yet know their mission. All Howard could tell them was that they had some 'special purpose'. Again they would drill. Again they would practice capturing and holding bridges. Howard had got these men into the best physical and mental shape of their lives.

Horsa landing marker and bust of John Howard.

Finally, towards the end of May, they were briefed on the true purpose of their mission.

Over the next few weeks men studied the maps and intelligence briefings of the landing zones... and they continued to practice.

At 2256 on 5 June, Howard's glider took off, followed at one minute intervals by the rest. Howard had been sick on every training flight prior to D-Day. As he sat in that great Horsa, gliding over France, he must have been nervous, he must have been worried, he probably thought through the plan over and over again.

Howard knew that a vital element in securing Bénouville Bridge was to destroy the pillbox position, near an anti-tank gun, within the first few moments of the landing. Pillbox positions always offered a considerable advantage to the defenders but, more importantly, the charges thought to be placed in the bridge would be blown from here. This last bit of information had come by way of informants in the vicinity, a Mr and Mrs Gondrée, who passed information to the Resistance in Caen. No.1 Platoon, the first to land, were given the job of neutralising the pillbox.

No.1 Platoon were also to secure the western side of the bridge whilst No.2 Platoon took the east. No.3 Platoon would reinforce No.1. Simultaneously to this, sappers would check the bridge for explosives and remove them, if required.

Over at Ranville Bridge the plan was an exact mirroring of this, using men from No.4, 5 and 6 Platoons.

Howard knew that he could not have prepared his men any better. As the glider neared its target he must also have thought about the good luck charm in his pocket: his two-year old son's little red shoe. Whatever had taken a grip of Howard's mind, on this flight he was not sick.

Howard was in the first glider with No.1 Platoon.

At 0014, the pilot, Staff Sergeant Jim Wallwork, called to Howard to get ready.

Wallwork had a tough job in the coming moments. He had to land accurately, try to destroy some of the barbed wire defences whilst doing so and, most importantly, try to keep the men alive.

All of the men in the glider, in keeping with their training, had linked arms with those next to them and raised their legs, waiting for impact.

At 0016, that impact came.

The landing was rough. Sparks were flying all around. Jim Wallwork and his navigator were thrown through the cockpit screen. Most men lay unconscious for a few moments. When Howard came around he initially thought he was blind… or dead; his helmet had been forced down over his eyes by the impact, thus giving the sense of darkness and disorientation.

A minute later the second glider landed right on top of a German trench.

Yet there was no enemy firing. No firing at all! The gliders had landed within metres of a German position and they had not been spotted. In fact, German troops had heard some noise, but they mistook it for the sound of an enemy aircraft being shot down.

Howard, now awake, aware and flooded with adrenaline, roused his men and, within seconds, they were charging towards the bridge.

As the third glider landed, Private Helmut Rother, a sentry on duty, suddenly saw Howard and his men galloping towards him. He turned, ran and shouted, 'Paratroopers!'

In the nearby Café Gondrée, Thérèse shook her husband, Georges, awake.

A German sentry fired a flare but it was his last action on this earth as a bullet slammed into him.

The important pillbox was neutralised with grenade and machine gun fire.

Liuetenant Den Brotheridge led the majority of No.1 Platoon across the bridge and threw a grenade into a machine gun position. Within seconds he was wounded by a bullet through the neck. Brotheridge later died of his wounds and became the first British soldier to die because of enemy action on D-Day.

Hearing the commotion, Georges Gondrée moved his wife and two daughters, Arlette and Georgette, into the cellar.

By 0026, a mere ten minutes after the first glider had landed, the bridge was under D Company's control. The engineers had checked the bridge and found that, although obviously prepared for them, the explosives had not yet been put into place.

The capture of Ranville Bridge had also been a success.

Lance Corporal Edward Tappenden sent out the coded success signal: 'Ham and Jam'.

Resistance had been light, for many of the *Osttruppen* had simply ran away. Two of them who should have been on duty were instead in a local brothel; Private Rother, along with another solider, simply hid in some bushes in which they stayed until they surrendered on D +1.

Again, the much vaunted *Wehrmacht* at the Atlantic Wall had melted away under the heat of battle.

But the evening was not over yet. Howard now had to hold the positions until relieved. At 0125 the first attempt to regain the bridge was made when two Mark IV tanks approached it. One was expertly dispatched with a bullseye shot using a PIAT (Projector, Infantry, Anti-Tank) that created a fantastic series of explosions. The other tank halted and withdrew.

By 0300 Lieutenant Colonel Geoffrey Pine-Coffin of the 7th Parachute Battalion and his paratroopers had managed to link

Café Gondrée.

up with Howard and his men. Throughout the night increasingly sustained sniper and machine gun fire from German positions pinned the paratroopers down. At one point Howard was shot at by a sniper. The bullet went through his helmet and sent him reeling. Many of the men thought he was dead, a belief seemingly confirmed by the flow of blood emanating from his wound and his immovable, unconscious state. However, he was only knocked out and somehow had suffered only a superficial injury. These are the fine margins in combat.[10]

They needed to hold until 1200 hours. This was the time that Lord Lovat and his commandos were due to arrive and link up with Airborne after their landing on Sword Beach earlier in the day.

At 1300 hours Howard spotted the indomitable figure of Lord Lovat, in his white pullover and grasping his walking stick, walking two paces behind Piper Bill Millin and with commandos in tow (See pages 128–30 for their landing on Sword Beach).

Over the next few minutes some of the most iconic scenes from D-Day played out. Georges Gondrée, ecstatic at the coming of the liberation, ran from his café and joyously handed out glasses of champagne to the troops. These were poured from the ninety-nine bottles that he had just dug up from his garden, hidden these last few years from the occupying Germans.

Still under fire and taking casualties, Lovat and the commandos crossed the Canal Bridge and headed to the River Orne whilst Bill Millin played his bagpipes – much to the utter amazement of all. But what a morale boost!

With the commando reinforcements, German resistance was eventually overcome and one of the most memorable missions of D-Day was over.

A reconstruction of a Horsa glider in the Pegasus Bridge Museum.

At 1600 hours, Winston Churchill announced to the House of Commons that the Bénouville bridges were in Allied control.

After the war Air Vice-Marshal Leigh-Mallory, the commander of Allied air forces, hailed the glider landings as *one of the most outstanding flying achievements of the war.*

Stephen E. Ambrose, acclaimed D-Day historian, commented that it would be hard to find a company that was better trained for any single mission in battle than D Company was on D-Day. Howard must take the plaudits for this; he was an inspirational leader

It is also important to remember the cost to the Germans of the loss of these bridges in the battles that ensued following D-Day. Their Panzer divisions were denied the most direct route to the invasion site and, instead, had to endure a near six-hour long detour around the severely bomb damaged city of Caen in order to engage with the Allied forces.

Those few men in their wooden gliders had helped make the liberation of Europe more likely to succeed than not. And, for that, it is worth us never forgetting what happened here.

Activities

Have a look at the information markers – they are on the exact position that each of the gliders came to a stop. There is also a bust of John Howard and the anti-tank gun is still in place. Walk across the bridge towards Café Gondrée (now Pegasus Café) and you are walking the route that Den Brotheridge and his men ran as they stormed the position just prior to Den receiving his fatal injury. However, the current bridge is not the original but an enlarged copy. The change was made in the 1990s to help with the flow of traffic and maritime vessels. The original is in the nearby museum.

The café itself is a magnet for battlefield tourists to the area and rightly so. Arlette Gondrée, a child at the time of the invasion and in the house on that night, is the current custodian, following the death of her parents. You will find her busily serving visitors most days. It is a wonderful place; full of nostalgic artefacts and, given its iconic status, simply a pleasure to say that you have been to it. Do remember, however, that it is a business rather than a museum and it would only be right to purchase a refreshment if you are planning to visit.

2a. Memorial Pegasus Museum

1 hour

The museum is easily located from the main battle site itself. It is well signposted and quite clearly visible.

Mémorial Pegasus
Avenue du Major Howard
14860 Ranville
Tel: +33 2 31 78 19 44
Fax : +33 2 31 78 19 42
info@memorial-pegasus.org
Lat & Long: 49.24208 -0.27185

Context

An outstanding museum which does a very good job of telling the Airborne story on D-Day and beyond. Contains a wealth of artefacts as well as a Horsa glider. There are a number of memorials and good audio-visual provision. Of course, perhaps most importantly, you can walk on the original bridge. I would highly recommend a visit if you have the time to do so.

The original Pegasus Bridge.

Sword, Juno and Gold 123

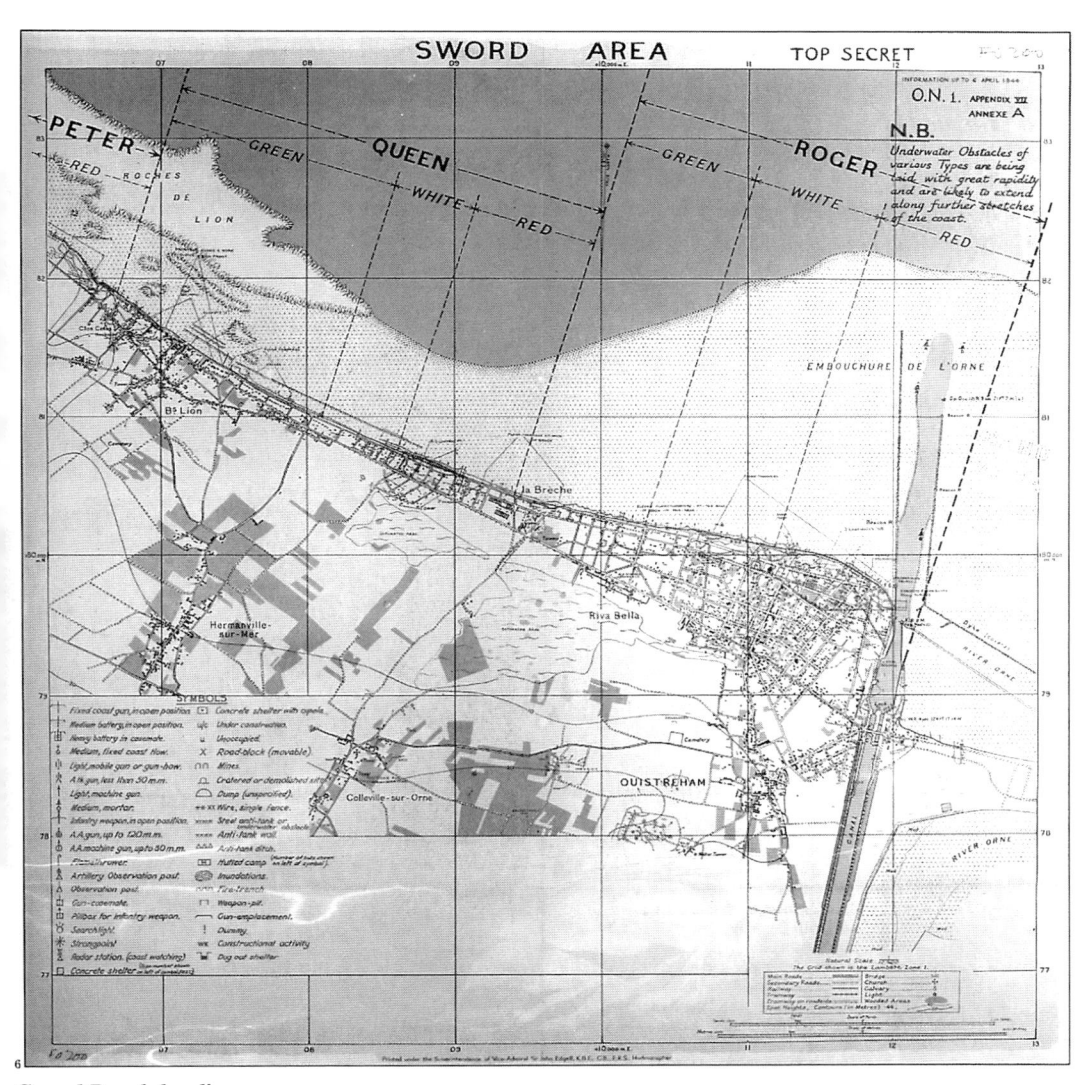

Sword Beach landing area.

British Operations at Sword Beach

Sword beach[11] was the most easterly landing beach on D-Day, stretching 8km from Ouistreham to Saint-Aubin-sur-Mer. The beach was divided into four landing sectors, (running from west to east): 'Oboe', 'Peter', 'Queen' and 'Roger'. Queen, a 2.9km section from Lion-sur-Mer to La Brèche d'Hermanville, was selected as the designated landing zone with 'White' and 'Red' beaches being the primary targets for the landing craft.

I Corps was assigned the task and it would fall on Major General Tom Rennie's 3rd Infantry Division to assault the beaches. The objectives were many and varied. 8th Infantry Brigade Group would be the first to land and after securing the beach, they were to relieve 6th Airborne at Bénouville Bridge. The 27th Armoured Brigade would support with tank units, many of which were 'Hobart's Funnies' with their various specialized variations. On the right of the landing, commandos from 41 Royal Marines Commando were to land at Luc-sur-Mer and link up with the Juno assault. No.4 Commando were to head east to Ouistreham whilst the 1st Special Service Brigade were also to get to Bénouville Bridge.

Major General Tom Rennie.

The landing at Sword had the most ambitious aim of all the landings on D-Day and was Montgomery's grandest plan for the day: troops from 185th Infantry Brigade were set the objective of leapfrogging the 8th Brigade, once the landing was secure, and to take Caen, 12km inland from the coast.

H-Hour was 0725.

The 8th Brigade were originally planned to be the final assault formation to land on D-Day.[12]

A naval bombardment preceded H-Hour and began at 0550.[13] A huge smokescreen had also been laid down by Allied aircraft in order to disrupt German surveillance out of Le Havre.

Crucially, DD tanks and other Landing Craft Tank-carried 'Funnies' were on the beaches before the infantry and so were able both to draw fire from German guns and support the assault immediately. Twenty-one out of twenty-five armoured vehicles or tanks made it ashore.[14]

The infantry arrived a couple of minutes after the designated H-Hour.

The German defences on Sword were reasonable, if not formidable. There were approximately twenty strongpoints across the whole of Sword, with strongpoint Cod facing directly on to the Queen sector. This was a system of trenches and bunkers with 50mm guns, mortars and machine guns. Merville Battery could, of course, potentially dominate the sector whilst snipers and mortars were peppered close to the beach itself. The typical barbed wire defences and mined sections of the Atlantic Wall were scattered across Sword too.

La Brèche translates as 'the breach' and is so named for a geographical feature, a dip at this section of the beach that leads inland to Hermanville. Major C. K. 'Banger' King, A Company Commander of the 2nd East Yorkshire Regiment, could not turn down the opportunity of reciting to the men on his landing craft the lines 'Once more unto the breach!' from Shakespeare's *Henry V*.

The initial landings went well, with nearly all the tanks making it ashore and the leading elements of 8th Brigade hitting the designated areas.[15] Initial German resistance was strong. This should come as no surprise: it is important to remember that the American assaults had begun an hour earlier; thus German troops were, if not certain of an attack, on extremely high alert. However, shortly before 1030hrs the main resistance was subdued and obstacles were being cleared. No.4 Commando, accompanied by elements of the Free French forces, were able to move on to Ouistreham whilst Lord Lovat's Special Brigade Service were heading for Bénouville.

As the day wore on, the major difficulty facing Sword was the rising tide. By noon the narrow beach strip measured only nine metres from seafront to water. Therefore, major delays and congestion dogged the follow-up landings throughout D-Day: an issue made worse by the fact that there was only really one suitable exit road from the beach.

Yet by 1400 hours the 185th Brigade were only 3km short of Caen. However, this rapid advance was checked by the leading elements of the 21st Panzer Division, who emerged north of Caen and up on the Périers ridge. For a short while this was a crucial moment for the Allied forces. There was still a gap between the British at Sword and the Canadians at Juno. If the Germans could repulse the 185th and then take advantage of this, then the success of D-Day could hang in the balance.

However, this threat never came close to reality due to the power of 'Firefly' Sherman tanks, equipped with 17-pounder anti-tank guns. Thirteen German tanks were knocked out for the loss of just one British tank. In addition, just before nightfall, a convoy of 250 British gliders passed overhead (heading for Bénouville); eyewitnesses reported this as a crushing blow to the morale of the German troops who were still attempting to repulse British infantry assaults. Shortly after this German forces pulled back to Caen itself.

Therefore, although Caen had not been captured, and would not be for another six weeks, a serious German counter-attack had been halted and another successful Allied footing on mainland Europe had been achieved.

2b. General Montgomery Monument, Colleville-Montgomery

15 minutes

From the Café Gondrée, head west on Avenue du Commandant Kieffer/D514 and at the roundabout take the 1st exit on to the D35. After 500m, turn left in order to stay on the D35, and drive for 3.5km. Then take the right on to Grande Rue/D60A and stay on this for 2.4km. The statue will appear on your right. Parking is available.

General Montgomery Statue
D60A
14880 Colleville-Montgomery
Lat & Long: 49.29043 -0.28213

Context

A quick stop en route to Sword Beach. Provides a good photo opportunity as well as a 'talking' stop on General Montgomery.

Orientation

On the way to this statue, you will have passed through the town of Colleville-Montgomery. Where this statue is situated is just a few hundred metres from Colleville-Montgomery Plage and the Queen Sector of Sword Beach, where the 3rd British Division made its way ashore. If you have time, it is worth heading to that sector of the beach for a few minutes after visiting this statue. Colleville-Montgomery was renamed after the war in honour of 'Monty'.

Narrative

See pages 48, 50–1 and 107 for information relating to Montgomery

Also:
Born in 1887, educated at St. Paul's School and Sandhurst before being commissioned in the Royal Warwickshire Regiment in 1908, Bernard Montgomery would go on to be one the most inspirational, heralded and, at times, frustrating, arrogant and difficult generals in the history of the British Army. He was brilliant. He was egotistical. And, as we all know, those with outstanding streaks often bring with them many quirks and flaws and arouse jealousies from those not quite as talented as they are.

During the Great War Montgomery served on the Western Front; shot through the right lung by a sniper during the first battle of Ypres in 1914, he spent the rest of the war as a staff officer, quickly rising up the ranks. His view on warfare in general was very much shaped by his Great War experience. He had no rose-tinted view of combat. It was bloody, it was tough and men die. Yet he also took away with him a visceral hatred for the squandering of lives. Therefore he tended to favour battle plans that were detailed and mapped out – almost set-piece in style – so that he could keep a close control over the men under his command and ensure that his resources were being deployed for the best possible reasons, rather than to simply fight for the sake of fighting.

During the inter-war years he held posts in various parts of the UK and its Empire and by the outbreak of the Second World War Montgomery was a major general. He was then given command of the Third Division of the British Expeditionary Force, which subsequently had to be evacuated from Dunkirk between May and June 1940.

From August 1942, he was in command of the British Eighth Army in the Western Desert until the Allied victory in Tunisia in May 1943. His victory at El Alamein (October-November 1942) is often seen as a turning point in the war because it was the first major defeat for the German Army.

He then commanded the British Eighth Army during the Allied invasion of Sicily and the advance into Italy before being recalled to Britain in order to take part in the planning for Operation Overlord.

Back in December 1941, at the Arcadia Conference in Washington D.C., a dual military command system between the British and Americans had been established. A crucial outcome of this was the decision that the Supreme Allied Commander for any theatre of war must have jurisdiction over all the forces in it, regardless of nationality. In 1943 General Dwight D. Eisenhower was appointed as Supreme Allied Commander Europe and, given the heavy American contribution, he was the natural choice to oversee Operation Overlord – leading the Supreme Headquarters Allied Expeditionary Forces (SHAEF). However, when deciding on the rest of the appointments, it was crucial to fully integrate British and American command. Both Winston Churchill and Franklin Roosevelt had wanted to appoint the (British) General Harold Alexander, the restrained, urbane and steady Commander-in-Chief, Middle East, as Commander-in-Chief Allied Ground Forces – a position of crucial importance to the success of D-Day. However, Alan Brooke (Chief of the Imperial General Staff) successfully lobbied against his appointment, making the case that Montgomery was a better general.[16] So it came to be that Montgomery would act as the commander on-the-ground, directing the battle for Eisenhower.

Alan Brooke (CIGS).

See pages 48–53 for planning D-Day

Many thousands of pages have been written about Montgomery. Yes, as previously mentioned, he could be a difficult man and he aroused much suspicion in those close to him. But he had that knack of winning and, ultimately, it is difficult to question that.

It is fair to analyse some of his grand 'master plans' a little more closely in order to understand the man and how war actually unfolds. Monty always claimed that his battles were designed, fought and unfolded to his own precise plans. Yet even the briefest study of D-Day, and the Battle of Normandy which followed it, would lead to the conclusion that this was a fanciful suggestion. Monty envisaged the capture of Caen on D-Day, followed by US First Army taking Cherbourg within a week. Then a British feint assault would occur east towards the River Seine, drawing the German forces in to a fight, whilst American troops broke out southwards. Whilst operations after D-Day developed, Monty claimed everything was unfolding to plan, even when this was clearly not the case. Thus he frequently clashed with Air Chief Marshal Sir Arthur Tedder (Deputy Supreme Allied Commander) and General Omar Bradley – even the easy-going Eisenhower threatened to remove Monty from command on more than one occasion.

On the other hand, Monty was captivating – he inspired devotion to the cause from his troops and, for all his self-promotion, stubbornness and difficulty, he

Monty.

got a great many important decisions correct. It was Montgomery who changed the initial invasion plans and expanded the landing area from three to five beaches, employing more manpower and resources. He also understood that the most crucial phase would be the landing itself, as the Germans, obsessed with the invincibility of the Atlantic Wall, would throw what they could into repulsing it rather than allowing the Allies to get established ashore. The liberation of Europe was dependent on the beachhead assaults.

On a personal level he was a magnetic, dominating personality. The actor ME Clifton James, who played Monty's double as part of Operation Copperhead,[17] studied the man closely, watching him speak, move, interact with others. He saw a compulsive man, completely inhabiting his own world; he was boyish at times, with avian-like mannerisms and who constantly pinched in his cheeks with his teeth. Much of the image was a construct but brilliantly done: the black beret that he wore was a self-conscious decision to distance himself from the rest of the 'brass-hat' generals and to solidify a connection with the rank and file. His raspy, high-pitched voice had a compelling quality to it. More than anything, James concluded that Monty was a natural – a showman, an inspirer… a force.

On 1 September 1944, Montgomery was promoted field marshal. After Normandy he commanded the 21st Army Group, which eventually succeeded in taking the port of Antwerp in Belgium but it was the failure at Arnhem that meant there was no short, sharp end to the war. His Army Group also fought during the Battle of the Bulge – Germany's last attempt to go on the offensive against the Allies.

Montgomery's forces crossed the River Rhine on 24 March 1945. On 3 May, Admiral von Friedeburg, Commander-in-Chief of the *Kriegsmarine*, arrived at Montgomery's German headquarters in Lüneburg in order to negotiate the surrender of the Third Reich to the Western Allies. Monty's greeting was quite typical of the man: 'Who are you and what do you want? I've never heard of you.' He then took the opportunity to berate von Friedeburg over the bombing of Coventry and Nazi treatment of the Jewish peoples of Europe, before then demanding an unconditional surrender. The next day the surrender was signed.

After the war, Montgomery was made a viscount, served as Chief of the Imperial General Staff and from 1951 to 1958 he was Deputy Supreme Commander of NATO forces in Europe. He died in 1976.

Perhaps Monty's finest hour was El Alamein. Yet for all his faults, the stubbornness, self-belief and absolute refusal to be defeated truly captures the spirit of the Allies in their fight to uphold freedom against tyranny.

Activities

Photo opportunity. A discussion over Montgomery's legacy and the internal politics and machinations of a command structure is often a productive exercise, given some basic understanding and appreciation of the complexities of military operations.

2c. Piper Bill Millin Memorial Statue, Sword Beach

10–30 minutes

Get back on to the D60A and drive towards the beach for a couple of minutes. The statue stands on your left and Sword Beach will be right in front of you.
Lat & Long: 49.29300 -0.28275

Sword, Juno and Gold   129

Context

A fitting tribute to a legendary D-Day story.

Orientation

The statue of Bill Millin is placed in front of the Queen Sector of Sword Beach, where the British 3rd Infantry Division and commandos of 1st Special Service Brigade came ashore on D-Day.

Narrative

Give an overview of the action on Sword Beach, pages 124–5.

Then:

William "Bill" Millin was the personal piper to Lord Lovat[18] on D-Day. Lovat's commandos were due to land on Sword approximately one hour after the first troops from 3rd Infantry Division came ashore. Their task was to sweep into Ouistreham, neutralising German defences in and around a former casino and eliminating the threat of battery fire upon further Sword landings. They then had to link up with the 6th Airborne Division at Bénouville in order to reinforce and secure the eastern flank of the invasion site.

At 0810 on D-Day, Piper Bill Millin was on LCI 519, standing just behind Lord Lovat. An LCT passed in the opposite direction, having just disembarked its tanks. Lovat asked Commander Rupert Curtis to hail her through the megaphone and ask how it went. A sailor called back, raising his fingers in a V-for-Victory sign: 'It was a piece of cake.'

Millin, hearing this, cast a glance at a burning LCT stranded on the beach, smoke rising in thick black fumes. He could see that men lay stranded on the beach – some digging in, others dead or wounded. This was a strange looking 'piece of cake'.

What was also strange was Bill Millin's very presence – most notably the fact that he had his bagpipes in hand. By the time of the Second World War, pipe playing in battle was an anachronism and limited by the War Office to rear areas only. When Lovat told Millin that he wanted him to be alongside him and play, he pointed out these restrictions. Lovat countered with: 'Ah, but that's the English War Office. You and I are both Scottish, and that doesn't apply.'

At 0835, LCI 519 came ashore and its ramps dropped. The commandos, all wearing their green berets, rather than helmets, were off. Almost immediately one man was eviscerated by shrapnel.

Lovat, stick in hand, wearing a white monogrammed pullover and beautifully polished brogues, strode into the water. On seeing how deep the water was upon the six foot Lovat, Millin soon followed behind, his kilt spread in the lapping waves, bagpipe against his shoulder and the sounds

Piper William 'Bill' Millin.

130 *Visiting the Normandy Invasion Beaches and Battlefields*

Lord Lovat.

of 'Highland Laddie' drifted over the battlefield.

Lovat and Millin made it to the top of the beach, linking up with others sheltering at the sea wall. Lovat was informed of Major Howard's success at the Bénouville Bridge, whence Lovat was to head with his men by 1200 hours. Lovat turned to Millin:

Piper 'Bill' Millin statue, unveiled in 2013.

'How about a tune?'
'What should I play then, sir?'
'The Road to the Isles', replied Lovat.

For the next hour, Millin roused the troops on Sword with his playing. Lord Lovat, looking just like the eccentric and brave aristocratic gent that he was, cheerfully greeted each subsequent wave of infantry as they made it to the top of the beach.

Allegedly German snipers thought that Lovat and Millin were insane, perhaps suffering some kind of mental breakdown under combat stress, and so did not fire at them. Whether this is true or apocryphal (i.e. they were just bloody lucky!) does not really matter: the whole episode stands as an incredible act of bravery, eccentricity and leadership. Lovat wanted Millin to play on that beach in order to instill a little more courage and fortitude in all those around them. For if a man could stride up and down Sword Beach playing a bagpipe and go unharmed, then surely this *was* a 'piece of cake' after all? No need to hunker down and hide; get moving off that beach and eliminate the enemy.

(See page 120 for Lovat and Millin at Bénouville Bridge).

Activities

A photo opportunity and a good place to discuss bravery and leadership and the value of displays of courage. It is, of course, quite something to walk on to the beach itself and take a few moments to contemplate.

* * *

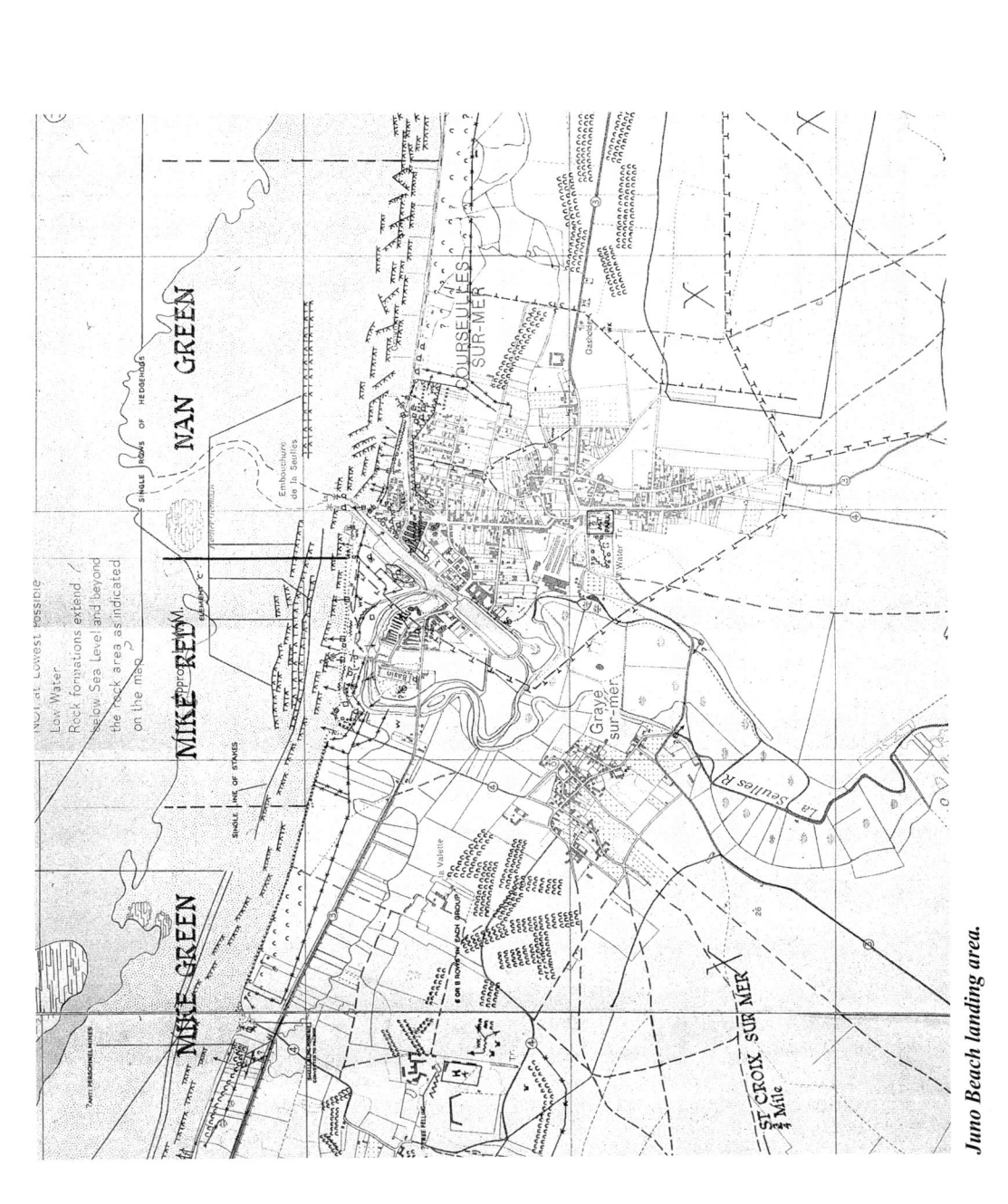

Juno Beach landing area.

Canadian and British Operations at Juno Beach

Juno Beach is a section of the D-Day landings area that runs for 9.7km from near la Rivière in the west to St. Aubin in the east.[19] The 3rd Canadian Division was given the task of assaulting this sector with the Canadian 7th Brigade at Courseulles and the 8th Brigade alongside them at Bernières. The 9th Brigade were held in reserve and would land later in the day. The 6th Armoured and 10th Armoured Regiments would offer tank support. 4th Special Service (Commando) Brigade would follow up the 8th Brigade landings. Overall, the Division consisted of 15,000 Canadians and 9,000 British personnel, led by Major General Rodney FL Keller.

The landing areas themselves were codenamed Mike and Nan and, as with the other beaches, were sub-divided into smaller sections. The Juno Beach assault was over a wide front (6km) and thus made the landing of two brigades feasible.

The objectives were: secure the immediate areas around Juno; clear and hold the nearby villages of Bernières, St. Aubin and Courseulles; aim for their furthest objective line – 'Oak' – the railway line close to the N13 road from Caen to Bayeux; capture Carpiquet aerodrome; and for 4th Special Service Brigade commandos to head east and link up with British forces at Sword.

Air reconnaissance just prior to D-Day highlighted problematic rocks close to the shoreline. As a consequence, H-Hour was delayed by ten minutes in order to allow the tide to rise and bring the landing craft in over the top of these obstacles.[20]

Task Force J, loaded with the 3rd Canadian Division, arrived offshore without trouble. HMS *Belfast* began shelling the German coastal positions at 0527, followed by the release of the landing craft some 12km from the beaches. The sea was rough and the wind high, which meant the landing was delayed even further as it took longer to cover the distance to shore. This meant that most tanks were brought in on LCTs although a few DD tanks did manage to drive in. Thus, as at the other British sectors, armoured support was available from the first landings – although, given the weather at Juno, the timetable was off target and the tank arrivals initially a bit haphazard.

One of the first major problems on Juno was the delayed landing; because of this the high tide had covered a large number of the beach obstacles which, subsequently, could not be identified as the craft came in. It is estimated that 30 per cent of all landing craft at Juno were badly damaged or destroyed, a major culprit being submerged Teller mines lashed on to wooden poles. Troops started to come ashore from 0745 and it took until 0815 for all of the troops from the two brigades to make it on to French soil.[21]

German resistance was strong, especially given the later landing time, for reports had already come in to the defenders at this sector of beach about the landings elsewhere. Heavy enfilade and mortar fire rained down upon Juno Beach and caused severe early problems. It would take two hours for Allied naval guns to fully silence the German Atlantic Wall positions at Juno.

Many troops coming in after the initial assault were taken aback by the sight of hundreds of men dead or injured on the beaches. What stuck in the mind of many on D-Day was the sight of corpses lapping up and down the beach in time with the tidal flows, bumping into one another like flotsam and jetsam from a demented other world: a ghastly but strangely hypnotic vision.

At 0845, 4th Special Service Brigade Commandos came ashore and immediately headed east towards Sword. Throughout the rest of the morning the 7th and 8th Brigade took part in intense street fighting around the villages of Bernières, St. Aubin and Courseulles. By mid afternoon all of the Canadian 3rd Division were ashore and the 9th Brigade was moving at a good pace inland.

By the end of D-Day the Canadians had linked up with the 50th (Northumbrian) Division to the west, a few miles south of la Rivière, and had managed to move further inland than any other Allied force when armoured units reached the Caen-Bayeaux road, 15 km inland. However, this objective was not fully established as the tanks had to withdraw later in the day due to outrunning their own infantry. To the east and southeast the 9th Brigade had not been able to take the Carpiquet Aerodrome due to stiff German resistance. Furthermore, the commandos had been unable to link up with the British 3rd Division at Sword, thus leading to a contested corridor of 3km between the two sectors, into which 21st Panzer Division attempted to counter-attack.

However, even after the partial tank withdrawal, the 3rd Canadian Division held the honour of advancing the furthest of all Allied divisions by the end of D-Day.

3. Bény-Sur-Mer Canadian CWGC Cemetery

30 minutes to 1 hour

Leaving the Piper Bill Millin Statue, turn left after the statue and then left again, before making two right turns in quick succession in order to head on to Rue du Commandant Kieffer. After 180m turn left onto Rue Georges Lelong before turning right onto the D514. Stay on this for 1.3km and then take the left onto Avenue du 6 Juin/D60B and turn right after 1km in order to stay on the D60B. After 1.5km turn left onto the D60 and 1.5km later take the right turn onto the D35. After 1.8km turn left onto Rue de Caen/D221 and stay on this for 2.6km. At the roundabout take the 2nd exit onto the D404 and stay on this for 5.4km. You will come to another roundabout; take the third exit onto the D35 and after 1km you will come to the cemetery on your right hand side.

Route de Reviers,
14470 Reviers.
Lat & Long: 49.30230 -0.45067

Context

In contrast to visiting battlefields of the Great War, I often visit only a handful of cemeteries when travelling with groups to the invasion sites of Normandy. This is partly because there are far fewer of them but also because of the abundance of preserved battlefield sites, memorials and the beaches themselves. However, I recommend this one as part of a main itinerary because, for me, it is a stunning place – everything that is so wonderful about the Commonwealth War Graves Commission and their work can be seen and admired in a place such as this.

An awe-inspiring, reflective and emotional place.

Orientation

The cemetery is 18km east of Bayeux and 15km north-west of Caen. It is 4km, as the crow flies, from Juno Beach itself. On D-Day there was a German battery position not far from here and Canadian troops had reached the village of Bény-Sur-Mer by late afternoon.

Narrative

This is Bény-Sur-Mer CWGC Cemetery. There are 2,048 burials here of which all but five are Canadian: 2010 Canadian Army, 15 Canadian Air Force, 3 British Army, 1 Royal Air Force and 1 French civilian. 19 burials are unidentified.

Then, read/give and account of the work of the CWGC (pages 33–6).

Bény-Sur-Mer CWGC Cemetery.

Then:

This cemetery was designed by PD Hepworth and has much in common with the pioneering designs of two of his predecessors as Principal Architects of the Imperial War Graves Commission after the First World War: Sir Edwin Lutyens and Sir Herbert Baker. You can certainly see the influence of Lutyens in the two watchtowers that feature so prominently here.

It is reasonable to assume that all the Canadians buried in this cemetery were volunteers. Because of considerable domestic political opposition, especially amongst the francophone population, when conscription was introduced service was confined almost exclusively to home service. To some extent this was a throw-back to the Pals' battalions of the Great War, where men joined up with their mates or work colleagues from their local areas. Therefore, there tended to be high concentrations of friends, colleagues and relatives in the same units. The Americans made an active effort to break up relatives and spread them around different units. The British Army had also endeavoured to do the same, given the terrible consequences felt during the Great War on small communities, devastated by loss. The Canadians had not done this. Therefore, astonishingly, in this one cemetery there are nine pairs of brothers and one set of three brothers.

The surnames of the pairs are: Blais, Boyd, Branton, Hadden, Hobbins, Meakin, Skwarchuk, Tadgell and White. The three brothers are named Westlake.

Most of those who are buried here died on D-Day or in the immediate days that followed. The Meakin brothers were killed on 8 June and their story is particularly tragic.

They were part of a group of over sixty Canadians who were taken prisoner during fierce fighting in the defence of the village of Putot-en-Bessin. Marched to the Château d'Audrieu, a headquarters for the fierce, obsessive and brutal 12th SS Panzer Division *Hitlerjugend,* they were murdered in cold blood – executed in batches in the grounds of the estate.

Just prior to the invasion, George had written to his mother back home in Birnie, Manitoba:

> 'This may be the last chance I get to write to you before the big day. If you don't hear from me for a while don't worry… Keep on smiling and everything will turn out for the best.'

Activities

Walk the cemetery and perhaps use this stop as an excellent opportunity to familiarize yourself (and/or your group) with how to use the Cemetery Register to locate graves by looking up the groups of brothers. As I state at the start of the book, I have tried to make this book as user friendly as possible and attempt to not go into too much detail about different regiments or units. However, every time I visit here with a group I am always asked, due to the intriguing name, what the Fort Garry Horse is – so it is worth me explaining this, just in case you experience the same – forewarned is forearmed! Initially the Fort Garry Horse was a cavalry unit that saw action in the First World War but by the time of the Second World War it was an armoured regiment – the 10th Armoured Regiment (The Fort Garry Horse). On D-Day their DD tanks came ashore with the 8th Brigade on Nan sector of Juno.

4. Juno Beach

10 minutes to 1 hour, depending on a quick visit or taking the opportunity to walk the beach a little.

Come out of the cemetery car park and turn right, back onto the D35. After 1km you will come to a roundabout, take the first exit onto Rue des Moulins/D170 and continue for 2.6km until you come to another roundabout – take the third exit onto the D79. After 800m, take the 2nd exit at the roundabout onto Rue Charles Benoist/D12. After 400m, turn left onto Avenue du Château and continue before turning left onto Quai E. After

Towards Juno Beach ...

a few hundred metres, turn left again onto Route de Ver/D514. After 450m turn right onto Rue de Marine Dunkerque and then take the right onto Voie des Français Libres. Continue until you come to the car park for the Juno Beach Centre.

Centre Juno Beach,
Voie des Français Libres,
14470 Courseulles-sur-Mer.
Lat & Long: 49.33618 -0.46099

Context

An opportunity to walk on Juno Beach and to visit the excellent Juno Beach Centre, should you have the available time.

Orientation

Head towards the sand dunes and you will soon be on Juno. You will notice a German command bunker, which was the main observation and control centre for German defences on this sector of Juno, which was named Mike Beach.

Narrative

Read/recount the story of the landings at Juno (pages 132–3)

Juno Beach.

Then:

It is important to consider the emotions that must have been coursing through the Canadians tasked with assaulting Juno on 6 June. Back on 19 August, 1942, elements of the 2nd Canadian Division had led an amphibious attack against the port of Dieppe that led to terrible losses. Although many lessons were learned for D-Day, it was poorly planned and a disaster in execution (see pages 44–5). Dieppe was a Canadian national disaster. Juno was revenge. It was on this beach that the most successful assault of 6 June took place. It is walking in the footsteps of men who should never be forgotten.

Activities

Walk the beach and have a look at the German bunkers.

4a. Juno Beach Centre

1 to 1.5 hours

Walk back to the Juno Beach Centre from the beach.

Centre Juno Beach,
Voie des Français Libres,
14470 Courseulles-sur-Mer.

Tel: +33 2 31 37 32 17
Fax: + 33 2 31 37 83 69
E-mail: contact@junobeach.org
www.junobeach.org

Context

A powerful, informative and immersive museum that covers (briefly) the history of Canada and of the contribution that Canada made to the Second World War. There are a number of themed rooms and also different temporary exhibitions throughout the year. What is particularly impressive is the extent to which the museum goes in order to engage with school-age visitors – utilising great narratives and modern technology, such as downloadable Apps, to do this. The student volunteer staff are superb and take great pride in their work. They are taking part in the Canadian Guide Program, which enables them to travel to France and work at the museum for one of three periods in a year. The shape of the building represents the Order of Canada and a maple leaf. There are a

The Juno Beach Centre.

Juno Beach Centre panorama.

number of striking memorials, sculptures and information panels and a great panoramic view can be had from the platform outside the museum.

'This is the beach where Canadian soldiers stormed ashore 59 years ago.'
Gareth Webb: D-Day veteran and founder of the Juno Beach Centre, 6 June 2003, at the official opening of the museum.

* * *

British Operations at Gold Beach

Gold Beach was the middle of the five invasion areas and had a width of 20km, stretching from Port-en-Bessin in the west to la Rivière in the east. As with all the beaches, Gold was subdivided into smaller sections: the main landing would take part on the Jig (Asnelles) and King (Ver-sur-Mer) Sections, an 8km stretch from le Hamel to la Rivière. XXX Corps commanded the assault with 50th (Northumbrian) Infantry Division tasked with carrying it out. 50th Division were a highly experienced formation, having already seen action at Dunkirk, the Middle East, North Africa and Italy during the war.

Troops from 231st Brigade would land at Jig and those from the 69th at King. 8th Armoured Brigade would provide tank support. 47 Royal Marines Commando would also land on Gold. 50th Division were led by Major General Douglas AH Graham, a man with a long and distinguished record of military service, who had been Mentioned in Dispatches on several occasions and received a Distinguished Service Order for his actions during the Second Battle of El Alamein. He was also the only senior British commander on D-Day to have previously taken part in an amphibious assault. This was a battle-hardened Division led by a highly experienced commander. Given this was the widest assault sector of the British beaches and second only to Omaha, tasking this stretch to such a formidable group was clearly well considered.

The beach was gentle, with no major obstacles at the top, but the sand was soft and AVREs would be required to lay matting in order to create a stable path for battle tanks.

Sword, Juno and Gold 141

The beach was defended by mainly poor quality *Osttruppen* troops of 716th Infantry Division and some more experienced troops from the superior 352nd. Approximately 2,000 German soldiers were stationed along the Gold Beach sector. However, *Kampfgruppe Meyer* – the 352nd Division's reserve and a mechanised unit – was held at Bayeux and, in theory, could be rapidly deployed in support. There were some concrete bunkers and strong points along the coast at Gold but they were fewer than in other sectors; instead, German forces tended to be concentrated in houses on the sea front. In addition were two artillery positions that had the potential to cause the Allies considerable problems. The first was a battery of four 122mm guns at Mont Fleury, although the position was not fully completed by 6 June. More formidable was a position on top of the high cliffs near to Longues. At this site, four 155mm guns were perfectly placed and very well protected by thick concrete emplacements.

The objectives were: secure a beachhead, take Arromanches, link with the Americans at Omaha and Canadians at Juno, capture Port-en-Bessin, split the N13 Bayeux-Caen road, capture the Longues Battery and seize Bayeux itself.

Vessels from Task Force G began to arrive off Gold Beach at 0530 on D-Day and the preliminary bombardment opened up at 0545. With H-Hour at 0725 this gave the guns a considerable amount of time to target German positions on this stretch of coast and, in comparison to other sectors, far more damage was caused. This was undoubtedly helped by the fact that many of the defences were based in regular housing rather than concrete emplacements.

However, the weather was particularly awful with four-foot high waves and a Force 5 wind. Battered and whipped about, men descended into their landing craft. The conditions caused many to bend double and vomit; so much so that men, years later, could never erase the sight and smells of a layer of sick slopping around their boots as they prepared to head to shore on that most fateful of days.

The DD tanks were supposed to hit the beaches a few minutes before the infantry but, due to the bad weather, they came ashore delayed by several minutes. Things did not get any better for the tanks, for when they did arrive, they were quickly bogged down by the extent of the beach defences that still remained intact. Because the demolition parties had

SYMBOLS

✝	Fixed coast gun, in open position.	⊡	Concrete shelter with cupola.
✝	Medium battery, in open position.	u/c	Under construction.
⌸	Heavy battery in casemate.	u	Unoccupied.
◊	Medium, fixed coast How.	X	Road-block (movable).
‖	Light, mobile gun or gun-how.	∩∩	Mines.
✶	A'tk gun, less than 50 m.m.	⌂	Cratered or demolished site.
●	Light, machine gun.	⌂	Dump (unspecified).
✚	Medium, mortar.	✳✳ xx	Wire, single fence.
●	Infantry weapon, in open position.	xxxx	Steel anti-tank or underwater obstacle.
⊕	A.A gun, up to 120 m.m.	xxxx	Anti-tank wall.

Gold Beach landing area

not yet arrived either, these tanks were picked off, hit mines or became stuck in the sand; there was only one flail tank that was able to support the first wave of infantry.

Layers of barbed wire and enfilade fire also met these first troops. Le Hamel offered stiff resistance, particularly coming from the Asylum at Asnelles. Troops in this building were able to direct machine gun fire on to the beach.

However, many of the other beach front positions were not that well defended and over the first hour many more tanks and men made it ashore. 'Hobart's Funnies' went to work clearing mines, laying material paths over the soft sand and bridging shell craters and anti-tank barriers.

La Rivière fell by 1000 hours and the Asylum at Asnelles was finally silenced by tank fire by midday. This meant that by early afternoon all of 50th Division's assault forces were ashore and ready to push on for their D-Day objectives. Due to pockets of stiff German resistance, not all of these were achieved. By nightfall No. 47 Royal Marine Commando were just outside Port-en-Bessin and thus had not yet established a link with the Americans at Omaha.[22] This was a major concern, as it left an exposed and vulnerable flank. Overall, the British had advanced 8km and were just short of Bayeux itself.

Most importantly, Arromanches had been captured and Gold Beach was secure: it could now be cleared in preparation for the installation of the artificial Mulberry Harbour that would be a vital supply line in the weeks and months ahead. HMS *Ajax* had silenced the guns of the Longues Battery.

One point to note, the much hoped for German 352nd Reserve mechanised formation had failed to show. Why? At 0400 hours they had been sent west towards Insigny in order to investigate reports of paratrooper landings. Then it was split and some headed to Omaha Beach and the majority returned to Gold Beach. However, they returned only in the late afternoon and were thus far too late to carry out any significant counter-offensive. They would, instead, be dragged into defensive fighting over the days ahead.

5. Gold Beach, King Sector, Stan Hollis VC

5–45 minutes, dependent on whether you are able/wish to travel down to the beach (tricky in a coach, easy in a car) or tell the story from the main road with a view of the position. It is, of course, better if you do head down the track, as you can then walk on to the beach itself.

Leave the Juno Beach Centre, heading north-west on Voie des Français Libres, then turn left onto Rue de Marine Dunkerque. After 250m turn right back onto the D514. Follow this for 4.7km. If you are going down to the beach and the Stan Hollis hut then you will need to take a right at an easy-to-miss and pretty indistinct crossroads. The right turn

The Stan Hollis hut.

is onto Herbage des Près but it is probably easier to keep an eye out for the sign for the left turn which points to Musée América Gold Beach on Avenue FD Roosevelt. When you do locate the correct turn (!), head down to the beach (or park if you are planning a brief microphone explanation on your coach). If heading down the track you will eventually come to a small hut. Park and walk over to the hut.

51 Voie du Débarquement
14114 Ver-sur-Mer
Lat & Long: 49.34525 -0.52802

Context

The exit road from King Sector beach and also an opportunity to tell the story of the only Victoria Cross winner on D-Day.

Orientation

From the D514 main road, the road down to the beach (Herbage des Près) is the exit road from King Sector. German defences were roughly where the D514 road is and a little further up the hill, thus giving excellent viewpoints over the landing troops. Approximately three-quarters of a kilometre further uphill was the Fleury Battery, the major German gun position in this sector.

Narrative

First, give an overview/read the general account of the Gold Beach assault (pages 140–3) or save it for when/if you walk on the beach itself.

King Sector exit road.

Then (assuming you have travelled down the minor road and are next to the Memorial to CSM Stan Hollis):

This is the beginning of the exit road from King Sector on Gold Beach. On all the landing beaches on D-Day, securing these exits/draws from the beaches in order that the advance of men and machinery could begin at once was of paramount importance. Any failure to do so could have left thousands of men stranded on the beaches and thus in a very limited zone and highly vulnerable to any sort of fire that the enemy could bring to bear; the invasion itself would have been in jeopardy.

Then explain the orientation, paying particular attention to the views that German positions had.

It is important to note that the land just behind this beach was particularly marshy, thus making the early assault even more problematic. It was the use of 'Hobart's Funnies' that proved to be particularly valuable here: flail tanks were able to clear minefields and provide cover for the advancing troops as they made their way up the rise in front of you and towards the enemy.

On 6 June, thirty-one-year-old Company Sergeant Major Stan Hollis came ashore here, at King Sector, on Gold Beach. Born in Middlesbrough, a former navigation officer for a Whitby shipping company, Hollis joined the Territorial Army in 1939. At the start of the war Hollis was sent to France, a member of the historic Green Howards (Yorkshire) Regiment. He was evacuated from Dunkirk, fought in North Africa and took part in the invasion of Sicily. But it is for his actions in Normandy that he is most remembered.

Hollis' invasion got off to a slightly farcical start. As he approached the beach in his landing craft, Hollis thought that he had spotted a German pillbox position. He unleashed a full drum of ammunition from his Lewis gun at this part of the famed Atlantic Wall. As he rushed on to the beach with men of the 6th Battalion of the Green Howards, he found the pillbox to be nothing more than this old tram hut that you see before you today. However, it is for his actions that followed this that he is most revered. Throughout the rest of D-Day Stan Hollis would prove himself to be a brave and courageous man, constantly putting the lives of others before his own. His VC citation best summarises his gallantry on that day:

Company Sergeant Major 4390973 (Warrant Officer Class II) Stanley Hollis's VC was announced in the London Gazette on 17 August 1944. His citation reads:

'In Normandy, France, on 6th June 1944, during the assault on the beaches and the Mont Fleury battery, CSM Hollis's Company Commander noticed that two of the pillboxes had been by-passed and went with CSM Hollis to see that they were clear.

When they were 20 yards from the pillbox, a machine-gun opened fire from the slit and CSM Hollis instantly rushed straight at the pillbox, firing his Sten gun. He jumped on top of the pillbox, recharged his magazine, threw a grenade in through the door and fired his Sten gun into it, killing two Germans and making the remainder prisoner.

He then cleared several Germans from a neighbouring trench. By his action he undoubtedly saved his Company from being fired on heavily from the rear and enabled them to open the main beach exit.

Later the same day, in the village of Crepon, the Company encountered a field gun and crew armed with Spandaus at 100 yards range. CSM Hollis was put in command of a party to cover an attack on the gun, but the movement was held up.

Seeing this, CSM Hollis pushed right forward to engage the gun with a PIAT from a house at 50 yards range. He was observed by a sniper who fired and grazed his right cheek and at the same moment the gun swung round and fired at point blank range into the house. To avoid the falling masonry, CSM Hollis moved his party to an alternative position. Two of the enemy gun crew had by this time been killed and the gun was destroyed shortly afterwards.

He later found that two of his men had stayed behind in the house and immediately volunteered to get them out. In full view of the enemy, who were continually firing at him, he went forward alone using a Bren gun to distract their attention from the other men. Under cover of his diversion, the two men were able to get back.

Wherever the fighting was heaviest CSM Hollis appeared and, in the course of a magnificent day's work, he displayed the utmost gallantry and on two separate occasions his courage and initiative prevented the enemy from holding up the advance at critical stages.

It was largely through his heroism and resource that the Company's objectives were gained and casualties were not heavier and by his own bravery he saved the lives of many of his men.'

In September 1944, Hollis was wounded in the leg and returned to the UK. In October, King George VI presented him his VC.[23]

CSM Stan Hollis.

Activities

The hut has further information regarding Stan Hollis on an information board. Just discussing the different topography of the beaches and inland positions tends to be useful, as by this stage your group will have an 'eye' for the different problems faced by the invasion forces on the various beach landings.

Then, if time, head down on to the beach itself (tide depending of course!).

5a. King Sector

Context

An opportunity to walk on the beach but also to consider another act of courage and fortitude.

Orientation

King Sector, Gold Beach. This is the spot where Stan Hollis landed along with the 6th and 7th Battalions of the Green Howards.

Narrative

As we have now seen, the Allied invasion of the Normandy coast line was a task of epic proportions, undertaken with much planning and with no certainty of success. As previously discussed (pages 51–3), pre-invasion intelligence operations were vital in order to mislead the Germans. Air reconnaissance and pre-war photographs of the beaches were also key aspects of building up as accurate a portfolio of information as was possible. However, this was not enough for Lieutenant Commander Nigel Willmott. It was his belief that to send thousands of men onto beaches with only the knowledge that photographs and charts could provide was ludicrous. What hidden dangers were lurking? Could the sand withstand the weight of the tanks? How did the sentries operate? He had studied the disastrous Gallipoli landing from the Great War; he had seen the problems of the Dieppe raid in 1942. It was following that debacle that Lord Louis Mountbatten[24] formalised Willmott's ideas and formed the highly secretive and specialist Combined Operations Pilotage Parties (COPP). Willmott was its commander.

Willmott was immediately tasked with somehow getting ashore and to attain as many samples of sand from the beaches as he could. However, by 1943 he was not particularly well and was certainly not fit for swimming in the sea, especially in winter: for that was exactly what was required.

COPP had approximately 200 servicemen, some of whom Willmott had trained in swimming at night from boat to shore. Commandos Sergeant Bruce Ogden-Smith and Major Logan Scott-Bowden were two of the very finest. When men ran ashore on 6 June 1944 they likely thought that they were the first Allied troops to set foot on these beaches. They were wrong.

King Sector.

Throughout the winter of 1943 and into the spring of 1944 Ogden-Smith and Scott-Bowden made dozens of expeditions to these beaches. Whenever there was a moonless night, they would be taken across the Channel by a small landing craft to within just a few hundred yards of the beach. They would then slip over the side of the boat and swim for shore. All they had with them was a torch, compass, waterproof writing tablet, equipment for collecting the samples and a fishing line. Plus, of course, a knife and a firearm – a .45 Colt, a weapon that seemed to be reliable even when wet and the barrel filled with sand.

Every time the two men undertook the mission the shock of the cold water permeating their wet suits would take the breath away. As they reached the beach they would lie flat and still... what could they see? Hear? Then the real work began. The fishing line was tied to a skewer and they would then ram this into the sand and unfurl it as they dragged themselves along their bellies up the beach. At intervals they would take and store sand samples, making a note of their location using their compass. Once they had collected enough they would use the line to work their way back to the water. They would then swim out to sea where they would tread water, shine their torches out to sea and wait until the landing craft came back to scoop them

Sergeant Bruce Ogden-Smith.

both up. The lack of a hundred per cent certainty that they would be retrieved must have been a devil of a psychological test.

This was, of course, an exceptionally dangerous mission. One night, on Omaha Beach, a German sentry tripped over the fishing line. Yet they were never caught. Both men were that mix of eccentricity and bravery that one finds in the British – not necessarily danger seeking but perhaps escapade embracing, reinforced by a strong dollop of endearing understatement.

On New Year's Eve 1943, Ogden-Smith and Scott-Bowden were on this exact stretch of Gold Beach. Whilst Scott-Bowden lay listening to the conversation of two German sentries, Ogden-Smith looked at his watch and noticed the time: midnight. He edged over to the Major and whispered: 'Happy New Year'. Little did he know then that it would be a great year for the Allies – one that was made all the more so because of the astonishing work of people such as them.[25]

Major Logan Scott-Bowden.

Activities

Beach walk; photo opportunity.

5. Asnelles, Gold Beach, Jig Sector

15 minutes

Leaving Stan Hollis's hut, head back up the minor road and turn right, back on to the D514. Stay on this for 4.1km. Just as you head into Asnelles, take a right turn onto Rue du Débarquement. After 200m you will come to the sea front. You will see a concrete gun emplacement/bunker and car parking. Park. *Note, if you are travelling in a large coach then these sea front roads are quite tight. It would be better to park in Asnelles and walk down any of the side streets to the beach front. If you are in a car, and have the time to take a more leisurely approach, then I would recommend parking in Asnelles town square, have a bite to eat at La Cale and walking down to the beach.*

Lat & Long: 49.34188 -0.58416

Context

An excellent site to see the remains of the Mulberry Harbour – to be recommended over the Arromanches beach due to the fact that Asnelles is simply much less busy.

Orientation

The concrete bunker was German position WN-37 and contained an 88mm gun. It was well positioned, having an excellent field of fire over Jig Sector of Gold Beach (as you look out to sea, to your right) where the 1st Hampshires landed. This was a particularly bloody stretch of beach for British troops on D-Day. If you look to your left and along the sea front, where housing lines the route, this is Item Sector of Gold Beach. No attempt to land troops was made on this area due to the high sea wall and considerable number of beach front houses – many of which contained snipers and machine gun crews. The 'Asylum' (see page 143) was also on this part of the sea front. Although that building has gone, most of the rest of the housing here today was there at the time of the invasion – you can see bullet holes and shrapnel damage on many of the exteriors.

WN-37.

Asnelles town square.

150 *Visiting the Normandy Invasion Beaches and Battlefields*

Now look back out to sea; whether the tide is in or out you will clearly see remains of the Mulberry Harbour.

Narrative

It is useful to give a version of the orientation of the site, then:

For most of our tour the focus has been on the build up to and then realisation of the invasion of these Normandy beaches. However, it is critical to remember that 6 June 1944 was just the beginning of something and it was not an end in itself. If this footing on French soil could be achieved, then it was merely the start of the slog to victory. In order to advance, the Allies were going to have to be able to bring many more men, machines, weapons and supplies over to the continent than they had on that day alone. Entire armies had to be brought to shore. This could not be achieved by landing craft. A large port was required.

None of the beaches chosen had anything like a port facility big enough for the envisaged supply operation. This had been one of the factors in choosing these sites – would the German command believe that the Allies would launch their major invasion assault across a stretch of coast where no large port existed? Arromanches, Courseulles, Ouistreham and Port-en-Bessin had small ports, but they were not up to the job. Cherbourg to the west and Le Havre to the east were ideal… but there was no guarantee of securing these in the space of time required in order to provide suitable supply networks. Besides, the Germans could destroy them once the invasion was underway as a precautionary measure.

In 1917, during the Great War, Winston Churchill had sent a brief memo to Prime Minister Lloyd George outlining an idea for an artificial harbour of some sort. He had been thinking about this concept for at least two years and had originally mooted it prior

Remains of part of the Mulberry Harbour.

to the ill-fated Dardanelles campaign. Twenty-five years later, Churchill returned to the idea.

On 30 May 1942 he sent a memo to Vice-Admiral Lord Louis Mountbatten: 'Piers for use on beaches. They must float up and down with the tide. The anchor problem must be mastered. Let me have the best solution worked out. Don't argue the matter. The difficulties will argue for themselves.'

The failure of the Dieppe raid in August of the same year only confirmed Churchill's opinion that capturing a harbour directly was fraught with problems. It might be possible to develop a plan where elite units could be deployed behind a major port, such as Le Havre, and attempt to capture it on D-Day. However, such an action would have been beset by a mass of military difficulties and would be a monumental gamble.

Winston Churchill.

Instead, the Allies proposed to bring their own harbours with them.

But how?

On 6 August 1943, Winston Churchill was on board the *Queen Mary*, travelling to Canada in order to attend the Quebec Conference with US President Franklin D. Roosevelt. Professor J. D. Bernal, a physicist working under Mountbatten, gave a scientific demonstration to his boss and the Prime Minister. It was held in a bathroom.

Bernal half-filled a bath and placed a couple of dozen paper boats on the water. He then asked a rather bemused naval lieutenant to make some waves using a loofah! The boats all sank.

The professor then repeated the experiment but this time he placed a mae west lifejacket around the boats. It did not matter how vigorous the naval lieutenant was with his loofah… the boats stayed afloat. Thus, the idea of the floating harbour was born.

Two weeks later at the Quebec conference the plan to develop two artificial floating harbours was given the green light. The War Office used the next available code-name from their official list. 'Mulberry' harbours they would be. The design and construction boffins had to make this happen within ten months.

And it did.

On the afternoon of 6 June the first elements of the Mulberry harbour left the UK and sailed toward France. The hope was to have two harbours, one on Gold Beach and the other at Omaha, ready within two weeks.

It was a simple but brilliant feat of ingenuity and engineering. To begin with, dozens of old ships would be sunk off the coast of all five of the landing beaches – these were coded 'Gooseberries'. They would provide an instant breakwater and thus calm the seas. In the initial days following D-Day this, in itself, made basic resupply using landing craft much easier. The next phase involved the sinking at Omaha and Gold of 146 'Phoenixes' – extremely large, hollow concrete boxes, or caissons, that were towed across from Britain. This, in effect, created a harbour wall. Finally, roads ('Whales') connecting the harbour wall to the shore were put in place over floating pontoons so that the undulations of the sea were absorbed. It still is quite amazing to contemplate the sheer genius of the realisation of that bathroom experiment just the previous year.

Mulberry 'A' at Omaha was destroyed during a severe storm on 19 June. Mulberry 'B', here at Gold, running in a huge arc from Asnelles to Arromanches and completed by 10 June, survived and became a vital life line for the Allies. It was used for ten months after D-Day, with 2.5 million men, 500,000 vehicles, and 4 million tonnes of supplies passing through it. The eventual capture of the port of Antwerp for the Allies meant that it was no longer necessary.

The other genius aspect to the Mulberry harbour plan was how beautifully it completely undermined the whole Atlantic Wall concept. Adolf Hitler had personally ordered its development, diverting millions of Deutschmarks, tonnes of concrete, steel and incalculable man-hours into its construction. He claimed that no invasion of mainland Europe would be able to succeed without the capture of a major port. Thus, every German held port on that coastline was defended like a fortress.

But every German port-fortress was ignored.

The Mulberry Harbour had once again proven that ingenuity, coupled with choosing to tackle the most difficult of challenges, can overcome even the most brutal looking of obstacles.[26]

Ingenuity: the genius of the Mulberry. Harbour.

Activities

If the tide is out then you can walk up to the remains of the harbour and have a close look. If time is not an issue then take a walk along the seafront and, if you have not done so, visit the little square in Asnelles (on the D514) itself. There are a number of interesting memorials as well as some good little shops and cafés. I would also recommend an unassuming looking little café called La Barak'a. You will find this as you drive out of Asnelles on the D514 heading towards Arromanches – super steak, outstanding seafood; at the time of writing, for the price you cannot go wrong at all.

6a. Arromanches 360°

1 hour

Rejoin the D514, the major road running through Asnelles, and continue in the same direction as you were travelling previously i.e. westerly. Stay on the D514 for 2.4km. You will see 'Arromanches 360°' on your right.

Arromanches 360°
Rue du Calvaire
14117 Arromanches-les-Bains
resa@arromanches360.com
Tel : 02 31 06 06 45
Fax : 02 31 06 01 66
www.arromanches360.com
Lat & Long: 49.33907 -0.61462

Context

Although I have refrained from inserting too many museum stops into the main itineraries – there are so many good ones that it feels unfair to discriminate – I have put this in as it works so well with groups, particularly younger ones. The main attraction is a fifteen minute, in the round, immersive and emotive cinema experience. Using archive photographs and video in tandem with dramatic voice-over and music, it really is something quite special. The film follows the build up to D-Day, the invasion, the Battle for Normandy and then all the way to the end of the war. Many of the groups I have taken, whether adult or student, have said that they felt much 'inspired' by the film. That sums it up best really.

Orientation

From the site you can clearly see down on to Arromanches beach.

Narrative

From outside the cinema you get excellent views over the beach at Arromanches. Therefore it is a good place to discuss Mulberry Harbours if you did not go to Asnelles (pages 150–3) or simply to expand on this a little further.

Some information on Arromanches itself may also be useful:

View out over Arromanches beach.

Sword, Juno and Gold 155

From this vantage point we can look down onto the beach at Arromanches. You will see remains of the Mulberry Harbour, which stretched from Asnelles to here. Today it is an extremely popular and busy coastal resort. On 6 June 1944 it lay just outside the western edge of the Gold Beach invasion area. Once the British forces had held and then advanced from the landing beaches, they turned toward Arromanches. Tanks of the 7th Armoured Division, in support of the 1st Hampshires and 1st Dorsets, first entered the town just after 1600 hours. German defence was strong. Although the Hampshires had gained control of most of Arromanches by nightfall, it was not until men of 47 Royal Marines Commando entered the fight on 7 June that the town fell into Allied hands completely. Without delay work began on the construction of the Mulberry Harbour.

Activities

Visit the cinema (best to have booked in advance – although individuals and small groups should be fine just to turn up and join the next showing, which is approximately every thirty minutes). The shop is also particularly well stocked. There are great viewing platforms outside as well as information boards, memorials and statues to provide further interest.

6b. Longues Battery

1 hour

Leave the Arromanches 360° car park, turning right and joining the D514. Stay on this for 1.2km. You will follow the road left and then turn right onto Avenue de Verdun/D514 and stay on this for 450m before talking the left onto Le Vailly/D514. You will come to

A gun casemate at the Longues Battery.

a roundabout, take the 1st exit and then stay on the D514 for 4.8km before turning right onto the D104. The battery site and car park will appear on your left.

Longues-sur-Mer Battery
Site de la Batterie
Rue de la Mer
14400 Longues-sur-Mer
Lat & Long: 49.34302 -0.69102

Context

Probably the best preserved German gun battery in Normandy today. Guns are still in situ and the whole site is full of interesting Atlantic Wall static positions.

Orientation

When standing at any of the gun casemates, Arromanches is approximately 8km east (to your right) and well within range, as was the naval armada off Gold Beach itself.

Narrative

Work began on the Longues Battery in September 1943. It is a large site that contains four gun emplacements, an observation bunker, other concrete defensive positions and was also home to anti-aircraft guns and searchlights. The guns were all 155mm calibre and, quite understandably, were a major concern for the Allied command. These guns had the potential to sink ships, wreak havoc on the beaches and hold up the invasion – particularly on Gold Beach.

In the hours before the invasion began, Bomber Command unleashed 1,500 tons of bombs onto the position. Yet, as you can see, the concrete was extremely thick and little effective damage was done.[27]

When the naval bombardment began these guns answered back and entered into something of a duel with HMS *Bulolo* and HMS *Ajax*. Over 100 rounds were fired onto the battery, which fell silent at 0845 hours. However, in the afternoon one of the guns began to fire again. The French cruiser *Georges Leygues* entered into a fierce fire fight with this last remaining gun until all fell silent again after 1800 hours.

Well over a hundred rounds were fired from Longues Battery on D-Day but the accuracy of fire was severely hampered by Allied bombs destroying the telephone cable between the guns and the advanced observation position. It is almost certainly the case that not one shell fired from here on D-Day hit an Allied ship. Many of the men who manned these guns were older (40+), not well-drilled in artillery operations, for they had spent the previous months working on finishing the construction of the site.

Troops of the 2nd Battalion The Devonshire Regiment attacked the battery on 7 June and succeeded in capturing the site, along with 184 prisoners.

Activities

This is a large site. Visit the concrete casemates but also follow the path down towards the cliff edge, where you will see an observation bunker, tower and many other emplacements. It is quite something to look out to sea from these positions and wonder what on earth must have been going through German soldiers' minds when they first caught glimpse of that spectacular Allied armada.

7. Bayeux CWGC Cemetery

30 minutes

From the Longues Battery, follow the one-way route to exit on the D104; stay on this for 1.3km before turning right in order to keep on the D104 for a further 4km. Then turn right, again staying on the D104 for 2.2km. At the roundabout, take the 1st exit on to Boulevard d'Eindhoven/D613 and stay on this for 1.1km. You will come to another roundabout at which you should take the 4th exit onto Boulevard du 6 Juin/D5A. Continue on for just over 1km, going straight on at a further roundabout. The road becomes Boulevard Fabian Ware and you will see the cemetery and memorial.

Lat & Long: 49.27441 -0.71409

Context

The largest CWGC Second World War cemetery in France and a fitting place to end a tour.

Narrative

If not previously discussed, then an ideal opportunity to discuss the work of the Commonwealth War Graves Commission (pages 33–6).

Then:

This is the Bayeux CWGC Cemetery. With 4,648 burials it is the largest British and Commonwealth Second World War Cemetery in France. It is a beautiful place. Across the road is the Philip Hepworth designed Bayeux

Their Name Liveth For Evermore …

Bayeux CWGC Cemetery.

Memorial to the Missing, which lists the names of 1,805 servicemen and women who lost their lives during the Battle of Normandy but have no known graves.

It is easy to get caught up in the excitement of the Second World War – the astonishing battles, tales of heroism and glory and of ultimate victory for the Allies. Yet we must remember that in order to defeat the tyranny of Adolf Hitler, men had to fight and many died doing so. Over fifty million people lost their lives during the course of the Second World War, most of those Russian. It is an impossible number to comprehend properly. The war lasted 2,174 days, which means that 23,000 died per day… or six per minute.

In George MacDonald Fraser's memoir of his experiences fighting against Japanese forces in Burma, he wrote a line that has always stuck with me. He said:

> 'With all military histories it is necessary to remember that war is not a matter of maps with red and blue arrows and oblongs, but of weary, thirsty men with sore feet and aching shoulders wondering where they are.'

Many men never made it home. It should be largely for them that we carry out these pilgrimages. It is for them that we take the time to walk in their footsteps and remember their sacrifices. What they did was incredible – they saved the world. For, as the Latin inscription on the Bayeux memorial says, with its nod to the history of 1066:

'We, once conquered by William, have now set free the Conqueror's native land.'

Activities

Walk the cemetery and look at the memorial. However, there are lots of interesting points to note here. The breakdown of nationalities is as follows: British – 3,935; Canadian – 181; Australian – 17; New Zealand – 8; Polish – 25; South African – 1; French – 3; Czech – 2; Italian – 2; Russian – 7; German – 466; Unidentified – 1.

It is interesting to note the different headstone shapes for some of the non-Commonwealth burials. There are burials ranging from brigadier downwards, which helps to convey the range of ranks who fought and died during the Normandy campaign. There is also a VC winner buried here: Corporal Sidney Bates (Headstone XX. E. 19). The citation for his award reads:

'In North-West Europe on 6 August, 1944, the position held by a battalion of the Royal Norfolk Regiment near Sourdeval was heavily attacked. Corporal Bates was commanding a forward section of the left forward company which suffered some casualties, so he decided to move the remnants of his section to an alternative position from which he could better counter the enemy thrust. As the threat to this position became desperate, Corporal Bates seized a light machine-gun and charged, firing from the hip. He was almost immediately wounded and fell, but he got up and advanced again, though mortar bombs were falling all round him. He was hit a second time and more seriously wounded, but he went forward undaunted, firing constantly till the enemy started to fall back before him. Hit for the third time, he fell, but continued firing until his strength failed him. By then the enemy had withdrawn and Corporal Bates, by his supreme gallantry and self-sacrifice, had personally saved a critical situation. He died shortly afterwards of the wounds he had received.'

Whatever you choose to do, it is a place where one can truly reflect on the magnitude, emotion and memory of your pilgrimage to the D-Day beaches and sites. You will never forget it.

* * *

– DAY END –

Footnotes:

1. Although many question this rather too neat post-war insight by Monty!
2. The 12th SS Panzer Division and Panzer Group *Lehr* were within a few hours' journey of Normandy and nine additional Panzer divisions within a day or two. In theory, 1,000 German tanks could have been brought into battle within twenty-four hours of the start of D-Day. Luckily for the Allies, the confusion and inertia in German command and control meant that this never happened.
3. Drop Zones for parachute and Landing Zones for gliders.
4. A sudden, surprise attack.
5. They actually turned out to be 100mm Skoda guns and 75mm French quick firing field guns from the Great War; however, these still would have been able to cause considerable damage and disruption and so this detail should not detract from the importance of the operation.
6. Largely wooden structure; could hold 30 men or they could hold equipment such as jeeps, anti-tank guns and ammunition, etc. They would be towed by cables attached to each wing (usually by Halifax or Dakota planes, but others too) and then released in order to make their near-silent landings. The idea was to be able to land men and equipment in a relatively small area whilst doing it with minimal disruption.
7. A soldier or airman assigned to a commissioned officer as a personal servant.
8. One had crash-landed in the UK when its tow rope broke shortly after take-off. The other had landed 8km away from Merville.
9. Many of the 'Germans' at Merville were actually Russian.
10. You can see the helmet in the Pegasus Bridge museum.
11. The codenames for the British beaches were selected from a list compiled by the British Army of words that were clear to radio operators even with extreme background battle noise. The American codenames were chosen by their generals.
12. This would not be the case due to timetable changes necessitated by the weather. Across the five sectors, troops on Juno Beach would be the final initial landings.
13. The only notable action by the German *Kriegsmarine* on D-Day occurred off the coast of Sword beach when torpedoes from an E-boat hit and sank the Norwegian destroyer *Svenner*.
14. It still remains a major question as to why the Americans did not use the same tactics on their beaches.
15. A note of some interest to those who enjoy the British obsession with drinking tea: the South Lancashire Regiment claim to have been brewing tea on Sword Beach by 0830hrs, thus making them the first to do so on D-Day. They would not be the last to do so: throughout the day, the opportunity to make a quick 'brew' was noted in all British and Canadian sectors. American troops often found this bizarre obsession of their Allied counterparts completely incomprehensible.
16. It is important to note that Montgomery was something of an Alan Brooke protégé.
17. A deception strategy to convince the Germans that Montgomery was in Gibraltar rather than preparing the Allied invasion of Europe.
18. Simon 'Shimi' Fraser, 15th Lord Lovat and Commander of 1 Special Service Brigade. He died in 1995.
19. Its initial codename was Jelly in keeping with the 'fish' names for the British sectors i.e. Goldfish, Swordfish and Jellyfish. Winston Churchill requested a change as he felt Jelly was far too undignified a name for an area of land that would see much bloodshed.
20. These 'rocks' turned out to be seaweed.
21. This is good pace for the offload of two brigades.
22. Their 16km advance was an impressive feat in itself. The Germans at Port-en-Bessin had offered extremely stiff resistance throughout the day and it would not be until 8 June that the commandos would take it.

23. Back in the UK, there is an excellent new (2015) statue honouring Stan Hollis that you will find close to the Middlesbrough Cenotaph, just outside the gates of Albert Park.
24. At this time head of Combined Operations.
25. Both men actually came ashore with the Americans at Omaha Beach on 6 June to act as guides, given their knowledge of the beach.
26. The other essential layer of infrastructure was a means to supply the huge quantities of fuel required to keep the invasion forces mobile. The solution was PLUTO (pipe line under the ocean).
27. The very badly damaged casemate that you can see was not caused by Allied shells on 6 June. This happened after D-Day and was the result of a tragic accident whilst it was being used as an RAF storage site. Ammunition exploded, killing four servicemen.

After D-Day

The success of D-Day was not absolute; it was however the first, essential, stage in the cracking of 'Fortress Europe'. The invasion and footing on mainland Europe had succeeded, but other objectives, such as the capture of Caen, had not been possible. Far from D-Day leading to a sprint to victory, fighting quickly bogged down in the weeks that followed. The 'battle of the *bocages*' – hedgerow to hedgerow fighting – was slow, bloody and frustrating.

Yet by August the Allies were approaching Paris and the Germans garrisoned there surrendered on the 25th. From here the Allies pushed German forces back through Belgium, the Netherlands and Luxembourg before the massive German counter-offensive in December at the Ardennes halted Allied progress.

However, this last gamble by Germany failed and by late January 1945 the Allies were able to reignite their offensive. At the same time, Soviet assaults continued to gather pace in the east and, bit-by-bit, German forces shrank back towards the Fatherland, squeezed on all sides by the rampant Allied forces.

On 20 April, Adolf Hitler committed suicide in his Berlin bunker and on 4 May Germany agreed an unconditional surrender.

With Germany out of the war, Allied forces now turned their attention to the defeat of Imperial Japan. Following the dropping of Atomic bombs on Hiroshima and Nagasaki, Japan surrendered on 15 August.

The Second World War was over.

For a more detailed timeline of events, see pages 7–12.

D-Day Museums

Find below a list of museums not directly referenced but in the immediate areas to the two itineraries covered in the book. In order to extend your tours then select a few of these excellent visits to add in.

UK

D-Day Museum and Overlord Embroidery
Clarence Esplanade
Portsmouth
PO5 3NT
Telephone: (023) 9282 6722

France

Arromanches:
Musée du Débarquement
The landing museum
Place du 6 Juin
14117 Arromanches
Tel. : +033 (0)2 31 22 34 31

Bayeux:
Musée Mémorial de la Bataille de Normandie
Memorial & Museum of the battle of Normandy
Boulevard Fabian Ware
14400 Bayeux
Tel. : +033 (0)2 31 92 93 41

Caen:
Le Mémorial, un Musée pour la Paix
The peace museum 'Memorial'
Esplanade Dwight D.Eisenhower
14066 Caen
Tel. : +033 (0)2 31 06 06 44

Carentan:
D-Day Paratroopers Historical Centre
D-Day Paratroopers Historical Centre/Dead Man's Corner Museum
2, Village de l'Amont
50500 Saint-Côme-du-Mont
Tel. (33) 2 33 42 00 42

Cherbourg:
Musée de la Libération
The liberation museum
Fort du Roule
50100 Cherbourg
Tel. : +033 (0)2 33 20 14 12

Douvres-la-Délivrande:
Musée Radar
The radar museum
Douvres-la-Délivrande (14440)
Tel. : +033 (0)2 31 06 06 45

Falaise:
Musée Août 44
August 44 museum
Chemin des Roches
14700 Falaise
Tel. : +033 (0)2 31 90 37 19

Grandcamp-Maisy:
Musée des Rangers
The Rangers museum
Quai Crampon
14450 Grandcamp-Maisy
Tel. : +033 (0)2 31 92 33 51

Musée de la batterie de Maisy
Maisy battery museum
Difficult to find. The following is advice from www.maisybattery.com.
'The site is hidden inside fields to the side of the D514.
The D514 is the main road which goes from Osmanville to Grandcamp-Maisy. As you enter Grandcamp you will see a sign for the town and we are located 200 metres after that down the road on the left. The road has a couple of different names… Routes des Perruques on some SatNavs – and just "Les Perruques" on others.'

Ouistreham:
Atlantik Wall museum
The Atlantik Wall museum
Avenue du 6 june
14150 Ouistreham
Tel. : +033 (0)2 31 97 28 69

N° 4 Commando museum
N°4 Commando museum
Place Alfred Thomas
14150 Ouistreham
Tel. : +033 (0)2 31 96 63 10

Port-en-Bessin:
Musée des Epaves sous-marines du Débarquement
D-Day wreckages museum
Route de Bayeux
Commes
14520 Port-en-Bessin
Tel. : +033 (0)2 31 21 17 06

Saint-Laurent-sur-Mer:
Omaha Beach museum
Omaha Beach museum
Rue de la Mer
14710 Saint-Laurent-sur-Mer
Tel. : +033 (0)2 31 21 97 44

Lotissement Omaha Centre
Overlord Museum
Rond-point du cimetière américain
14710
Colleville-sur-Mer
Tel.: +033 (0)2 31 22 00 55

Sainte-Marie-du-Mont:
Musée du Débarquement
Landing museum
Sainte-Marie-du-Mont (50480)
Tel.: +033 (0)2 33 71 53 35

Ver-sur-Mer:
Musée América – Gold Beach
America Gold Beach museum
Place Amiral Byrd
14114 Ver-sur-Mer
Tel. : +033 (0)2 31 22 58 58

Going further, doing more

The following section gives a few recommendations for extending your tours further. The main itineraries are good for easily two or three days and the obvious first choice for extending your trip is to select from the museum section. However, if you are 'museumed-out' or have got the 'battlefield-bug' then perhaps try some of the following places.

I have given an indicator of roughly where you would add these stops into the main itineraries. Furthermore, I have assumed that if you are going to add these sites then you will be somewhat more confident with the history and touring and will be carrying out your own research to suit your interests. Therefore, I have only added a very brief description of what one will find at the site/memorial/cemetery.

Additions to Tour One:

After 1a.
Iron Mike' US Parachutist Monument, La Fière
La Fière was the scene of heavy fighting during the early hours of D-Day. American paratroopers seized a vital causeway over the flooded surrounding land. The statue is a stunning tribute and memorial for all American Airborne forces who took part in D-Day.

After 1b.
Utah Danish Memorial
Close to the Dick Winters' statue, this memorial commemorates the 800 Danes who were a part of the D-Day landings. Most were attached to British units and served on board ships.

After 2.
Brecourt Manor Band of Brothers Memorial
You will find a memorial to the actions undertaken at the Brecourt Manor assault (see page 69) just off the D14. The assault itself was just past the memorial in the tree line ahead of you. The nearby large farm complex is the Manor itself. However, please do not go into the farm or on the land surrounding it as this is private property.

Carentan
Those familiar with the *Band of Brothers* story will be aware of this town. The Germans held it until 11/12 June. It is also the site of the first major assault carried out by a link-up between American forces from Utah and Omaha. There are a couple of memorials near the town hall, which itself is also worth a visit due to the flags, plaques and items

of interest from the visits of US veterans over the years. The town is also a good stop for a bite to eat.

Additions to Tour Two:

After 1.
Ranville CWGC Cemetery
A beautiful place, perhaps most notable for the burial of Lieutenant Den Brotheridge (see page 119).

After 2
Caen
Horrendous carnage and destruction was brought upon the civilians of Caen during the Battle for Normandy, both from the Allied aerial bombardment and the fighting that followed. Over a thousand were killed in the two major air raids on it, many more were casualties and thousands fled the city. Caen itself was a first day objective for the British but it was not actually captured until August. Very little of the pre-war city remains today and the need for rebuilding work was so extensive that it was not completed until the 1960s. If you are planning to visit the excellent Peace Museum, then some time in Caen itself is also recommended, even if just for a refreshment or shopping stop.

This stop could be built in at any time you are in the Sword Beach area.

HILLMAN Strongpoint, Périers Ridge
The site of the strong German position which had briefly caused trouble for the Allies on D-Day. (See page 125). Use *rue du Suffolk Regt* on your Satnav.

After 2c.
Churchill Tank/No 41 Royal Marine Commando Sundial Memorial, Roosevelt Quotes – Lion-sur-Mer
Taking the D514 coast road toward Juno Beach you will pass through Lion-sur-Mer and will not be able to miss the striking Sundial metal shafts that rise into the sky. Commandos were used to link up between major beach sectors on D-Day in order to keep the flanks connected. These interesting memorials are on the site of 41 Commando's successful assault on the afternoon of D-Day.

Lion-sur-Mer.

After 3
La Déliverande CWGC Cemetery
Another impressive cemetery, which is in the vicinity of the Douvres Radar Station Museum, which you might also wish to visit.

Courseulles
On your way to the Juno Beach Centre you may wish to have a stop in this seaside town. There are quite a

number of interesting memorials, one of the most famous being that of the site of General de Gaulle's landing here on 14 June. You will also see a Sherman tank.

After 6a.
Arromanches
If it is not the height of summer when you visit (or you do not mind being swamped with tourists), then I would recommend visiting the town of Arromanches itself. There is an excellent museum as well as shops and refreshments plus the obvious draw of walking on to Gold Beach itself and getting up close to the Mulberry Harbour.

After 7.
Bayeux
A beautiful city and the first major town liberated. There is much to see and do here (the Bayeux Tapestry being an obvious general interest stop) and it is a wonderful place to spend some R+R after your busy touring day(s).

* * *

Bayeux.

Further Resources and Web Links

All those books and websites listed below were vital research works for the author. I would highly recommend each and every one of them to you:

Guide Books

Evans D, *A Guide to the Beaches and Battlefields of Normandy*, Amberley Publishing, Gloucestershire, 2010.
Holt T and Holt V, *Major and Mrs Holt's Definitive Battlefield Guide D-Day Normandy Landing Beaches,* Pen & Sword Military, Barnsley, 2014.
Hughes G, *Visiting the Somme and Ypres: Battlefields Made Easy*, Pen & Sword Military, Barnsley, 2014.
Kilvert-Jones T, *Normandy: Sword Beach – 3rd British Division/27th Armoured Brigade,* Pen & Sword Military, Barnsley, 2000.
Kilvert-Jones T, *Omaha Beach: V Corps' Battle for the Normandy Beachhead*, Pen & Sword Military, Barnsley, 1999.
Reed P, *Walking D-Day*, Pen & Sword Military, Barnsley, 2014.
Saunders T, *Gold Beach Jig Sector and West*, Pen & Sword Military, Barnsley, 2002.
Shilleto C, *Pegasus Bridge and Merville Battery: Normandy*, Pen & Sword Military, Barnsley, 1998.
Shilleto C, *Normandy: Utah Beach – VII Corps and 82nd and 101st Airborne Divisions*, Pen & Sword Military, Barnsley, 2000.

Histories, Biographies and general reference

Ambrose S E, *Band of Brothers*, Simon & Schuster, London, 2001.
Ambrose S E, *Citizen Soldiers: US Army from the Normandy Beaches to the Bulge, to the Surrender of Germany, June 7, 1944 to May 7, 1945,* Simon & Schuster, London, 1998.
Ambrose S E, *D-Day*, Simon & Schuster, London, 2013.
Ambrose S E, *Pegasus Bridge*, Simon & Schuster, London, 2002.
Ashcroft M, *Special Forces Heroes*, Headline Review, London, 2008.
Beevor A, *D-Day: The Battle for Normandy*, Penguin, London, 2014.
Ferguson N, *The War of the World: History's Age of Hatred*, Penguin, London, 2009.
Gilbert M, *Churchill's War Leadership*, Random House, London, 2004.

Hastings M, *All Hell Let Loose: The World at War 1939–1945*, Harper Press, London, 2012.
Hastings M, *Overlord: D Day and the Battle for Normandy 1944*, Pan, London, 2012.
Holmes R, *Fatal Avenue*, Vintage, Croydon, 2008.
Johnson B, *The Churchill Factor: How One Man Made History*, Hodder, London, 2015.
Johnson P, *Churchill*, Viking Press, USA, 2009.
Joll J, *Europe Since 1870*, Pelican, 1976.
Keegan J, *Six Armies in Normandy: From D-Day to the Liberation of Paris June 6th – August 25th, 1944,* Pimlico, London, 2004.
Kershaw I, *Hitler*, Penguin, London, 2009.
Langworth R, *Churchill's Wit: The Definitive Collection*, Ebury Press, Chatham, 2009.
Lee S J, *European Dictatorships 1918–1945*, Routledge, Cornwall, 2016.
Mayo J, *D-Day Minute by Minute*, Short Books, London, 2015.
Rankin N, *Churchill's Wizards: The British Genius for Deception, 1914–1945*, Faber and Faber, London, 2009.
Roberts A, *A History of the English-Speaking Peoples since 1900*, Phoenix, London, 2007.
Roberts A, *Masters and Commanders: The Military Geniuses Who Led the West to Victory in WWII*, Penguin, London, 2009.
Roberts A, *The Storm of War: A New History of the Second World War*, Penguin, London, 2010.
Sheffield G, *Forgotten Victory – The First World War: Myths and Realities*, Headline Book Publishing, London, 2002.

Websites

http://americandday.org – American focused; full of first-hand accounts and documents.
http://battlefieldsww2.50megs.com/ – Military historian and battlefield guide Paul Reed's excellent WW2 site.
http://www.ddaymuseum.co.uk/ – Website of the Portsmouth museum; contains a very fine history section.
http://www.dday-overlord.com/eng/normandy_landing.htm – A fine general interest site.
http://www.historyofwar.org/ – as described: an on-line vast resource of military history info.
https://www.iwm.org.uk/visits/d-day75
http://www.pegasusarchive.org/ – superbly detailed and full of first-hand accounts of the Pegasus raid.

Acknowledgements

My love of battlefield touring goes back to my own school days and to two wonderful trips that left an indelible imprint upon me. In my previous book I gave a lengthy thanks to those brilliant teachers at Silcoates School who, in a bizarre twist, became, for a short time, my colleagues. I offer a grateful nod once again to Les, Tom, Franksy and, of course, Nige.

Following in their footsteps, to be a part of the world of teaching continues to be an absolute pleasure. This is, of course, made all the more enjoyable when you work with outstanding colleagues. Many thanks go to Adam Hall, Callum Braidwood-Smith and Ed Long for their support, encouragement and routine 'robust banter'. I count myself extremely lucky to have had the good fortune to spend my work hours alongside people I am proud to call great friends. I would also like to thank Laura Powell and Louise Clarke for their support on our trips over recent years – I can only apologise for having to put up with us: what on earth did you do to deserve it!

Pen & Sword Books are brilliant. With the ink barely dry on my *Visiting the Somme and Ypres* book, I energetically pitched the idea of a D-Day follow-up to Henry Wilson at P&S. 'Could I complete it within a year,' he asked – of course, not a problem… over double the amount of time later, and thus way overdue, the manuscript finally appeared. Life, the day job, plus a myriad other bumps in the road meant that this book became both simultaneously a labour of love and, at times, of utter frustration.

This was the non-fiction writing equivalent of the difficult second album.

Yet the great people at P&S were constantly supportive, moving their timeline to fit in with me. How could anyone ask for a better publisher? So, special thanks to Henry Wilson and Matt Jones for their patience and to Jon Wilkinson for designing another quite beautiful cover.

Jonathan Webb continues to offer much helpful support, always the first to ask how far behind I am at that moment in time or when the book is coming out and then laugh, a lot, before handing over another beer.

I would once again like to thank Paul Bennett for his generosity in giving time to check my manuscript and his erudite and perceptive suggestions for improvements. My approach to writing is to just go for it – scatter gun and trail of thought with ideas and points developing as I go – Paul is brilliant at pointing out appalling grammatical errors and incredible inconsistencies in my original drafts. He helps to shape the mess into something semi-ready…

… And Nigel Cave is the master at turning it into a fully formed and coherent work. Nigel is outstanding. I always think that he must look at some of my work and just want to tut and shake his head – his knowledge is so superior to mine that I feel like an imposter in the battlefield world. Yet he never once makes one doubt themselves. His ideas and suggestions for improvements have been just superb. He has scribbled points in the margins that have sent me off on the most wonderful of research tangents. He will not let any shabby history through his Cave-filter and I am most, most grateful for that.

My father, a truly wonderful man and inspiration to me, passed away in early 2017. We shared battlefield trips together and retraced the steps of my grandfather on the Somme battlefield on many occasions. Dad brimmed over with love, generous humour and positivity; it was he who enabled all of this to happen by providing such an encouraging and supportive upbringing. I miss you Dad – thank you for everything.

Thank you also to my beautiful children for putting up with such a boring and constantly distracted Daddy – I can only apologise. And… Samantha – I will never be able to explain properly what you mean to me or how much I have to thank you for: you are my best friend and the greatest support anybody could ever wish for. I love you x

Finally, I would like to once again thank my students – especially those who have been on one of my 'tours' (and their parents who enable it to happen!). You continue to inspire me just as much as, I hope, the history inspires you.

Gareth Hughes, March 2019

Index

82nd Airborne Division, 59, 63, 65, 72, 102
101st Airborne Division, 54–5, 59, 63, 69–70, 72, 102

American Battle Monuments Commission (ABMC), 36-7
Arromanches 360°, 153–5

Bayeux CWGC Cemetery, 36, 157–9
Bény-Sur-Mer Canadian CWGC Cemetery, 133–6
Bradley, Gen Omar, 48, 50, 69, 84, 127
Brécourt Manor assault, 69–70, 166

Canham, Col Charles, 83–4
Churchill, Winston, 7–8, 10, 12, 24, 26, 28, 30–1, 34, 48–9, 51, 121, 127, 150–1, 160
Commonwealth War Graves Commission (CWGC), 33–8
Composition of armies, 5–6
Cota, Brig Gen Norman, 83–4, 104

D-Day:
 after D-Day, 162
 Allied planning, 48–53
 American airborne operations, 59
 British Airborne operations, 107–109
 British Army operations, 107
 deception, 51–3
 decision to go, 53–5
 glossary, 39–42
 Juno Beach *see* Juno Beach main entry
 Omaha Beach *see* Omaha Beach main entry
 Osttruppen troops, 47, 71, 117, 120, 141
 Pegasus Bridge *see* Pegasus Bridge main entry
 Sword Beach *see* Sword Beach main entry
 Utah Beach *see* Utah Beach main entry
Dieppe, 29, 44-5, 138, 147, 151

Easy Company *see* Winters, Richard
Eisenhower, Dwight, 40, 42, 48–51, 53–4, 63, 127

First World War, 13–14

Gale, Maj Gen Richard, 107–109, 117
German War Graves Commission (Volksbund Deutsche Kriegsgräberfürsorge), 37–8, 76–7
Gold Beach:
 Asnelles, 148–50
 British Operations, 140–3
 Jig Sector, 148–53
 King Sector, 143–8
 map, 142
Great War *see* First World War

Hitler, Adolf:
 Mein Kampf, 19, 23, 25–6, 32 n.9
 NSDAP, 19–20, 41
 preparations for Allied invasion, 44–8
 responsibility for war, 24–6
 rise to power, 16, 18–21
 steps to war, 21–4
Hollis, CSM Stan, 143–6
Howard, Maj John, 115–22, 130

Imperial War Graves Commission (IWGC) *see* Commonwealth War Graves Commission (CWGC)
Inter-war years, 15–24

Jahnke, Lt Arthur, 74
Juno Beach:
 beach, 136–8
 Bény-Sur-Mer CWGC cemetery, 133–6
 Canadian and British Operations, 132–3
 map, 131

La Cambe German Cemetery, 76–8
Longues Battery, 42, 141, 143, 155–7
Lovat, Lord (Simon Fraser), 92, 109, 120, 125, 129–30

Maps:
 Gold Beach, 142
 Juno Beach, 131
 Merville Battery, 110
 Omaha Beach, 80
 Operation Neptune, 56

Pegasus Bridge, 115
    Sainte-Mère-Église, 60
    Sword Beach, 123
Merville Battery, 42, 106–107, 109–14, 116, 124
    map, 110
Millin, Piper Bill, 92, 120, 128–30, 133
    memorial statue, 128–30
Montgomery, FM Bernard, 6, 48–51, 53, 107, 125–8
    monument, 125–8
Mountbatten, Lord Louis, 44–5, 49–50, 147, 151
Mulberry Harbour, 40, 99, 143, 149–55, 168

Normandy:
    pre-war, 43
    under occupation, 43–4
Normandy American Cemetery and Memorial, 37, 76, 79, 99–103

Ogden-Smith, Sgt Bruce, 147–8
Omaha Beach:
    American Operations, 81–5
    Dog Green Sector, 94–9
    map, 80
    Pointe du Hoc *see* Pointe du Hoc main entry
Otway, Lt Col Terence, 110–14

Patton, Gen George S., 40, 48, 52, 98
Pegasus Bridge, 2, 115–22, 160
    Memorial Pegasus Museum, 122
Peregory, Sgt Frank D., 79, 102
Pointe du Hoc, 79, 81, 85–94, 104

Reagan, Capt Ronald, 90–4
Ridgway, Maj Gen Matthew, 59, 62–3, 93
Rommel, FM Erwin, 8–9, 11, 45–8, 50, 52–3, 55, 73–4, 97

Roosevelt, President Franklin, 8, 10, 12, 28, 30–1, 48–9, 72, 127, 151
Roosevelt, Quentin, 103
Roosevelt Jr, Brig Gen Theodore, 72, 74, 102

Sainte-Mère-Église, 59, 60–8, 72
Scott-Bowden, Maj Logan, 82, 147–8
Second World War:
    causes, 13–24
    Fortress Europe, 44–8
    historiography, 24–6
    overview, 26–31
    timeline *see* Timeline of the war
Stagg, Group Capt James, 53–4
Steele, Pte John 'Buck', 65–6
Stresemann, Gustav, 18, 21
Sword Beach:
    British Operations, 124–5
    Map, 123

Taylor, A.J.P., 24–5
Taylor, Col George A., 83
Taylor, Maj Gen Maxwell, 59, 63
The Statue of Peace, 78–9, 85
Timeline of the war, 7–12
Treaty of Versailles, 13, 15–17, 21–5, 37

US Airborne Museum, 67–8
Utah Beach:
    American Operations, 71–2
    museum, 72–5
    overview, 72–5

Volksbund Deutsche Kriegsgräberfürsorge *see* German War Graves Commission
von Rundstedt, FM Gerd, 45–7

Willmott, Lt Cmd Nigel, 146–7
Winters, Lt Richard 'Dick', 67–70, 72, 166